The Special School's Handbook

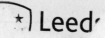

The Special School's Handbook gives an up-to-date picture of the work of special schools, using case studies of good practice to provide clear suggestions on how special schools may be further developed.

This practical and informative book provides an invaluable and timely companion for anyone teaching or planning to teach in special schools in the United Kingdom. Wide-ranging chapters address topics such as:

- Adapting the curriculum to give special schools more flexibility
- Implications of Every Child Matters and multi-professional working
- Organisational changes in special schools
- The changing roles of staff in the modern special school
- Ways of assessing the progress and achievement of pupils
- Working with parents.

Each chapter features thinking points and suggestions for further study.

The Special School's Handbook contains a wealth of invaluable information, resources and advice for all staff working in or supporting special schools, parents whose children attend them and anyone interested in the work of the modern special school.

Michael Farrell is a special education consultant, working with schools, local authorities, voluntary organisations, universities and others in Britain and abroad. He has published extensively in the area of special education.

Other titles from Routledge by Michael Farrell

Key Issues in Special Education: Raising Standards of Pupils' Attainment and Achievement
Hb: 978–0–415–35423–3, Pb: 978–0–415–35424–0

In this highly practical book, Michael Farrell unpicks and clarifies the role of educational standards in today's schools, drawing extensively on detailed, real-life case studies.

Celebrating the Special School
Pb: 978–1–84312–407–8

The book celebrates the success and importance of special schools within England and the support of local education authorities (LEAs) in maintaining them.

The *New Directions in Special Educational Needs* Series by Michael Farrell comprises the following titles:

Dyslexia and other Specific Learning Difficulties Pb: 978–0–415–36040–1
Autism and Communication Difficulties Pb: 978–0–415–36039–5
Behavioural, Emotional and Social Difficulties Pb: 978–0–415–36038–8
Moderate, Severe and Profound Learning Difficulties Pb: 978–0–415–36041–8
Sensory Impairment and Physical Disability Pb: 978–0–415–36042–5

By focusing firmly on what really works in practice with children with special educational needs, this highly practical series will enlighten and inform any busy teacher eager to know more about individual difficulties, and who wants to make inclusion a reality for their pupils.

Related titles from Routledge

Commonsense Methods for Children with Special Educational Needs (5th edition)
Peter Westwood
Hb: 978–0–415–41581–1, Pb: 978–0–415–41582–8

'At a time when many practitioners are still (naturally) wary of including children with special educational needs in their mainstream classrooms, this down-to-earth book will help to build confidence, dispel prejudice and allay fears. It should be on the shelves of all school and faculty of education libraries.' Christina Tilstone, Senior Lecturer, University of Birmingham

Interactive Play for Children with Autism
Diana Seach
Hb: 978–0–415–35373–1, Pb: 978–0–415–33326–9

Easily accessible, and packed full with practical resources, this comprehensive guide discusses the shared play experiences that assist in the development of communication, social understanding and cognition among children with autism.

Available at all good bookshops
For ordering and further information please visit:
www.routledge.com

The Special School's Handbook

Key issues for all

Michael Farrell

Routledge
Taylor & Francis Group

LONDON AND NEW YORK

nasen
Helping Everyone Achieve

First published 2008
by Routledge
2 Park Square, Milton Park, Abingdon, Oxon OX14 4RN

Simultaneously published in the USA and Canada
by Routledge
711 Third Avenue, New York, NY 10017

Routledge is an imprint of the Taylor & Francis Group, an informa business

© 2008 Michael Farrell

Typeset in Garamond by
Florence Production Ltd, Stoodleigh, Devon

British Library Cataloguing in Publication Data
A catalogue record for this book is available from the British Library

Library of Congress Cataloging in Publication Data
Farrell, Michael, 1948–
    The special school's handbook: key issues for all/Michael Farrell,
        p. cm.
    Includes bibliographical references and index.
    1. Children with disabilities – Education – Great Britain –
    Handbooks, manuals, etc.   2. Special education – Great Britain
    – Handbooks, manuals, etc.   I. Title.
    LC4036.G7F373 2007
    371.90941–dc   2007001863

ISBN13: 978–0–415–41685–6 (hbk)
ISBN13: 978–0–415–41686–3 (pbk)
ISBN13: 978–0–203–94577–3 (ebk)

nasen is a professional membership association which supports all those who work with or care for children and young people with special and additional educational needs. Members include teachers, teaching assistants, support workers, other educationalists, students and parents.

nasen supports its members through policy documents, journals, its magazine *Special!*, publications, professional development courses, regional networks and newsletters. Its website contains more current information such as responses to government consultations. **nasen**'s published documents are held in very high regard both in the UK and internationally.

Contents

Illustrations

Plates

Figures

Boxes

The author

Having trained as a teacher and as a psychologist (Institute of Psychiatry, Maudsley Hospital, London), Dr Michael Farrell taught pupils with a wide range of special educational needs. He has worked as a head teacher, a lecturer at London University, and as an LEA inspector for special education. After managing a national project at City University, he directed a project for the then Department of Education and Employment, developing materials and course structures for teacher education. He is currently a special education consultant with local authorities, schools, voluntary organisations, universities and others both in Britain and abroad.

Author of many articles and books on special education, among his recent publications are: *Standards and Special Educational Needs* (Continuum, 2001); *The Special Education Handbook* (3rd edition) (David Fulton, 2002); *Understanding Special Educational Needs* (Routledge, 2003); *Special Educational Needs: A Resource for Practitioners* (Sage/Paul Chapman, 2004); *Inclusion at the Crossroads: Special Education – Concepts and Values* (David Fulton, 2004); *Key Issues in Special Education: Raising Standards of Pupils' Attainment and Achievement* (Routledge, 2005); *New Directions in Special Educational Needs* (series of five books) (Routledge, 2006); *Celebrating the Special School* (David Fulton, 2006).

Author with Harry the bulldog

Preface

A government White Paper in 2005 mentioned special schools frequently (DfES, 2005a) claiming they would be at the heart of the system and speaking of money being allocated to upgrade special school buildings. In 2006, the DfES announced it was providing start-up funds for a national representative body for special schools – the Federation of Leaders of Special Schools. The body was intended to allow a collective voice for special schools; offer additional training to special school staff; share best practice; and help special schools work more closely with mainstream schools for the inclusion of pupils with SEN. The Federation brings leaders together regionally and nationally and has involved a number of organisations in its development including the National Association of Emotional and Behavioural Difficulty Schools (NAES), the National Association of Independent Schools and Non-maintained Special Schools (NASS), the National Association of Headteachers (NAHT) and Entitlement and Quality Education for Pupils with Learning Difficulties (EQUALS).

Yet as long ago as 1997, a government Green Paper (consultation document) announced that:

> The ultimate purpose of SEN provision is to enable young people to flourish in adult life. There are therefore strong educational, as well as social and moral grounds for educating children with SEN with their peers. We aim to increase the level and quality of inclusion within mainstream schools, while protecting and enhancing specialist provision for those who need it.
>
> (DfEE, 1997: 43).

Later, guidance showed a lack of evenhandedness when responding to parents expressing a preference for either a mainstream or a special school for their children. The document *Inclusive Schooling: Children with Special Educational Needs* (DfES, 2001b) gives statutory guidance on the framework for inclusion under the Education Act 1996 as amended by the Special Educational Needs and Disability Act 2001. The guidance states:

The Act seeks to enable more children who have special educational needs to be included successfully within mainstream education. This clearly signals that where parents want a mainstream education for their child *everything possible should be done* to provide it. Equally, where parents want a special school place their wishes should be *listened to and taken into account*.

(DfES, 2001: 1 para. 4, italics added)

The government's 'Strategy for SEN' applying to the period 2004–5 (DfES, 2004c) commented: 'We believe that special schools have an important role to play within the overall provision for children with SEN – educating some children directly and sharing their expertise with mainstream schools to support greater inclusion' (ibid.: 2.12). When the document mentions movement between mainstream and special sectors, it tends to mean movement of pupils from special to mainstream. The document states: 'We also want to see more pupils moving between the sectors, using annual reviews of children's statements to consider the scope for a dual placement or transition to a mainstream school' (2.13).

Furthermore, 'the proportion of children educated in special schools should fall over time as mainstream schools grow in their skills and capacity to meet a wider range of needs' (2.15). Also, 'a small number of children have such severe and complex needs that they will require special provision' (2.15). But, 'children with less significant needs – including those with moderate learning difficulties and less severe behavioural and social needs – should be able to have their needs met in a mainstream environment' (2.15).

The Strategy uses phrases such as 'having their needs met' without specifying what those needs are or how it would be known if they were met. It does not specify that pupils are best educated in a school where their educational progress and personal and social development is enhanced. It restricts the vision for special schools as being for pupils with the most severe and complex difficulties, not for pupils who would receive a better education and develop better there.

In 2006, an OfSTED report *Inclusion: Does it matter where pupils are taught?* (OfSTED, 2006) examined factors promoting good outcomes across different provision for pupils with 'learning difficulties and disabilities'. The survey on which the report was based took place from 2005–6 and involved 11 inspectors making visits of two days to 74 schools in 17 local authorities, visiting mainstream schools, resourced mainstream schools, special schools and pupil referral units. The survey found 'effective provision' to be equally distributed between special schools and mainstream schools when 'certain factors' were in place. More good and outstanding provision was found in resourced mainstream schools than elsewhere. Characteristics considered in judging schools to be effective were academic and vocational achievement; personal development; and social development. Important factors were the ethos of the school; specialist staff; the focused professional development of all staff; and flexibility and responsiveness to individual needs. It appears from the list of schools at the end of the report that 20 special schools in England were sampled.

Also in 2006, a government website was still proclaiming about having needs met (not about providing the best education) and about special schools being for pupils with the most severe and complex needs instead of being for children who would progress better in them than in mainstream schools:

> The government expects the proportion of children educated in special schools to fall as mainstream schools develop the skills and capacity to meet a wider range of needs. A small number of children have such severe and complex needs that they will continue to require special provision, but children with less significant needs – including those with moderate learning difficulties – should be able to have their needs met in a mainstream environment.
>
> (www.everychildmatters.gov.uk/ete/specialschool)

A report *Special Educational Needs* (House of Commons Education and Skills Committee, 2006) highlighted government confusion and muddle in special education. The minister responsible for special education is quoted in evidence to the committee saying that the government 'have no policy whatsoever, I should stress, of encouraging local authorities to close special schools' (ibid.: 6). The report asks, if this is so, then why do some local authorities 'believe they have been instructed to close special schools' (ibid.). The report itself unfortunately is confused in taking pupils who are gifted and talented to have special educational needs (e.g. ibid.: 16) although it does not explain what disability or difficulty in learning a child has that enable him or her to become, for example, an outstanding pianist. The report does point out that research on whether children with similar special educational needs and cognitive ability achieve better in a special school, a mainstream school or elsewhere is limited and that the 'limited research that does exist is inconclusive' (ibid.: 19).

Throughout this time, special schools throughout England have continued with their work, often unrecognised, at times derided by lobby groups depicting special schools as oppressive and divisive.

But the tide was turning. It was as though the realisation had dawned that it was not too politically incorrect to risk saying that schools are about helping pupils to learn something and trying to show that they have done so. The complaints about the 'standards agenda' from some quarters seemed suddenly to be rather like people complaining about there being a 'meteorology agenda' for weather forecasters or the terrible prospect of there being a 'building agenda' for architects. In other words, it has come to be recognised that the primary goal of schools is education and that that cannot be bought off by extremist lobbyists pressing for some distorted notion of inclusion.

Parents' groups began to mobilise to protest against proposed closures of special schools. Mary Warnock (2005) criticised certain politicians, ministers and civil servants involved in lowering the esteem in which special schools are held. She maintains that mainstream schools can be settings in which children with SEN can be isolated, marginalised, unhappy and disaffected. More recently, she has stated, 'I profoundly believe that for many children, not only those with the most severe or multiple disabilities, special schools are their salvation' (Warnock, 2006: viii).

Innovations are taking place in special schools up and down the country as a few examples involving NASS illustrates. A pilot project of the school improvement partners approach was evaluated by Leadership for Learning at Cambridge University and involved seven local authorities, 24 maintained special schools and two non-maintained special schools. In 2006 NASS was involved in a project with the University of Northampton and the Foundation for People with Learning Difficulties seeking to better respond to special school pupils having mental health needs. The Association has also run a project on outreach from independent and non-maintained schools resulting in a series of exemplars giving guidance on how schools can meet the challenges of new special school roles.

Exciting developments are apparent in maintained special schools across the nation as the many examples in this book indicate. Yet as inclusion gives way to education as the central value of schools, good special schools must continue to build their reputations as centres of excellence. This is why it is important that they continue to find ways of improving.

I hope that the present book might help special schools and others with this aspiration.

Michael Farrell
Epsom
March 2007
dr.m.j.farrell@btopenworld.com

Acknowledgements

I would like to thank the special schools, local authorities, universities, charitable bodies, organisations and others who provided information that helped in the preparation of this book. I am also most grateful to the following colleagues who kindly read earlier versions of chapters and made invaluable comments. Chapter 2: 'Organisation and structure' Liz Turnbull, Headteacher, Hadrian School, Newcastle. Chapter 3: 'Outreach and other roles' Nancy McArdle, Headteacher, Thomas Wolsey School, Ipswich, Suffolk. Chapter 7: 'Target setting' Liz Bull, Headteacher, Slated Row, Milton Keynes. Chapter 8: 'Multi-professional working' Nick Byford, Headteacher, St Piers School, Surrey. Chapter 9: 'Home–school partnerships' Jane White, Headteacher, Broadfield School, Lancashire. Chapter 11: 'Funding' Michael Thompson, Headteacher, Hexham Priory, Hexham, Northumberland.

My grateful thanks go to Alison Foyle and the team at Routledge for their support and encouragement throughout.

Over many years and for several of my publications, including the present one, the staff of Epsom library have provided an excellent service retrieving for me documents from specialist libraries and resource centres throughout Britain and elsewhere and I would like to express my warm thanks to them.

I am grateful to the parents, children and to the schools for the photographs. The photographs are children from Aspley Wood School, Nottingham; Bidwell Brook School, Devon; The Lyndale School, Wirral and Rosewood School, Southampton.

Ruth Hunt (www.flickr.com/photos/kitti) took the picture of the author and bulldog 'Harry'.

Abbreviations

ADHD	attention deficit hyperactivity disorder
AFASIC	Association of All Speech-impaired Children
ASD	autistic spectrum disorder
ASDAN	Award Scheme Development Accreditation Network
BARE	Below Age Related Expectations
BESD	behavioural, emotional and social difficulties
BILD	British Institute of Learning Disability
CAF	Common Assessment Framework
CD	communication difficulties
CPO	Child Protection Officer
CSCI	Commission for Social Care
CYPSP	Children and Young Persons Strategic Partnership
ECM	Every Child Matters
EQUALS	Entitlement and Quality Education for Pupils with Severe Learning Difficulties
EY	Early Years
IAPC	Institute for the Advancement of Philosophy for Children
ICT	Information and Communications Technology
IE	Instrumental Enrichment
IEP	Individual Education Plan
ITT	initial teacher training
LSA	Learning Support Assistant
MDVI	multiple disability and visual impairment
MLD	moderate learning difficulties
MOVE	Mobility Opportunities Via Education®
NAES	National Association of Emotional and Behavioural Difficulty Schools
NAHT	National Association of Headteachers
NASS	National Association of Independent Schools and Non-maintained Special Schools
NC	National Curriculum
NCYPE	The National Centre for Young People with Epilepsy

NMSS	Non-maintained Special Schools
NPPN	National Parent Partnership Network
NSF	National Service Framework
P4C	philosophy for children
PEC	Picture Exchange Communication System
PESSCL	Physical Education, School Sport and Club Links
PFI	Private Finance Initiative
PfS	Partnership for Schools
PIVATS	Performance Indicators for Value Added Target Setting
PMLD	profound and multiple learning difficulties
PPA	planning, preparation and assessment
PSHCE	Personal, Social, Health and Citizenship
RNIB	Royal National Institute for the Blind
SCRIP	South Central Regional Inclusion Partnership
SEN	special educational needs
SENJIT	Special Educational Needs Joint Initiative for Training
SERSEN	South East Regional Special Educational Needs Partnership
SLD	severe learning difficulties
SMSA	School Midday Supervisory Assistant
SPELL	Structure, Positive, Empathy, Low arousal Links
SSA	Specialist Support Assistant
SWOT	strengths, weaknesses, opportunities, threats
TDA	Training and Development Agency
TEACCH	Treatment and Education of Autistic and related Communication-handicapped Children
YPSS	Young People's Support Service

Ball

Chapter 1

Innovative organisation

This chapter examines various approaches to organisation and structure that a special school can develop in collaboration with other schools and with the local authority. I look at the collocation of special schools and mainstream schools; dual registration/placement; extended schools including 'full service' schools and children's centres; federations that include special schools; and the specialist special schools programme (along with the leading-edge partnership programme). The chapter explores organisational issues surrounding the development of generic special schools. In both the opportunities provided by the closer location of special and mainstream schools and in organisation of generic special schools, I suggest that account is taken of the progress and development of pupils.

Collocation

A special school and a mainstream school may be 'collocated' on a campus, or even more closely positioned within the same complex of buildings, allowing opportunities for pupils to learn together, as the example of Vale School in Haringey demonstrates (see Box 1.1).

If the principles of optimal education (Farrell, 2006f: 14–26) were to apply, the areas of the curriculum pupils experienced would be monitored so that the pupil spent the optimum amount of time in the mainstream and the special school to encourage the best academic progress and personal and social development. This could range from all the pupil's time being spent in special school, all of it being spent in mainstream school or varying proportions in each, but the proportions of time would be based on evidence of the pupil's progress and development.

The 'Building Schools for the Future' programme aims to replace or renew all secondary schools by 2016 to 2021, subject to future spending decisions. One outcome of the programme is that special schools and ordinary schools may be brought physically closer (www.teachernet.gov.uk/management/resourcesfinanceandbuilding/schoolbuildings/sbschoolsforthefuture). Such

Box 1.1 VALE SCHOOL, HARINGEY

Collocation

Vale School, Haringey is a co-educational day community special school for 85 pupils aged 2 to 19 years having physical disabilities and has purpose-built 'resource bases' (accommodation and facilities) on the same sites as two local schools, Lancasterian Primary School and Northumberland Park Community School (a secondary school). At both sites, Vale School has its own classrooms, therapy areas, offices and other facilities. It also has the opportunity to include some children part-time or full-time in the mainstream classrooms, both sites being accessible to wheelchairs. There are also opportunities at another local infant and junior school allowing up to 16 pupils aged 5 to 11 years to be included full-time in mainstream classrooms with the support of Vale teachers, therapists and visiting professionals from other agencies.

Vale has access to various professionals including physiotherapists, speech and language therapists, occupational therapists, dietician, school nurse and peripatetic specialist teachers for visual impairment and hearing impairment. Staff in consultation with parents determine the extent of inclusion in mainstream classrooms, pupils' progress being a significant factor in determining where pupils are taught.

Various professionals support the Vale resource base for pupils aged 2 to 11 years at Lancasterian School where pupils require the specialist base for most of their learning. The Vale resource base at Northumberland Park School houses the administration, secondary and post-sixteen departments, offering opportunities for pupils to obtain qualifications including the ASDAN (Award Scheme Development Accreditation Network) Youth Award Scheme, GCSEs and (if they use a communication aid) the City and Guilds Effective Augmentative Alternative Communication Certificate. Vale School also provides advice and consultancy to mainstream schools to support teachers educating pupils with a physical disability.

Box 1.2 THOMAS BEWICK SCHOOL, NEWCASTLE UPON TYNE

'Building Schools for the Future'

Thomas Bewick School, Newcastle upon Tyne is an LEA-maintained community special school educating 64 children and young people aged 3 to 19 years with autistic spectrum disorder. It is organised into foundation stage, primary, secondary and sixth form departments as well as a weekly residential unit accommodating up to 10 children, allowing a 24 hour curriculum. Among less usual forms of accreditation, the Mencap Gateway Award is being piloted at Key Stage 3.

Staff are trained in nationally accredited courses: the Picture Exchange Communication System; TEACCH (Treatment and Education of Austistic and related Communication-handicapped Children); and Team Teach. Several teachers are studying for the part-time distance-learning course in autism through Birmingham University and others are attending postgraduate courses (Master of Arts) at Northumbria University. Staff have completed in-house training in autism awareness and in curriculum development in relation to autism (both taught by Northumbria University); Makaton; effective communication; and autism and ADHD. A full-time speech and language therapist is based at the school.

Part of Newcastle LEA's involvement in 'Building Schools for the Future' is the development of a new school building for Thomas Bewick where it will share a campus adjacent to Beech Hill (a mainstream primary school) and All Saints Church of England College (a mainstream secondary school). The new special school, scheduled to open in March 2008, will educate up to 90 pupils from preschool age to 19 years. It will provide a base to support early multi-disciplinary assessment, identification and assessment for preschool children and will have a resource centre to support families. The school will support additionally resourced centres and individual pupils with autism who are taught in mainstream schools, by outreach. Through links with the University of Northumbria and Newcastle University, the school will operate as a centre for educational research and development. It will also provide in-service training for teachers, teaching assistants, parents and staff from agencies other than education.

In preparation for the new school, a working group was formed of parents, governors and senior teachers and a consultant (ex-adviser) working on behalf of the school. Consultation took place with parents and pupils about what they would like in the new school. The school looked at forms of new buildings found in the centre of Newcastle and made an exhibition of findings and preferences in Newcastle Central Library. It also held consultations with parents and others.

The working group required many meetings with the architects and design teams to talk about what the school needed for pupils with autism. Since it is an all-age provision, the school asked that the building would have contrasting phase provision for the pupil's journey through the school so that there was a clear difference in each phase of their learning from early skills and knowledge learning on to learning to be an independent adult. It was also required that areas in the school were secure and safe for the pupils. There was always the emphasis that the school style was to be a confident statement and not a building hiding away. Also important was the need for pupils to work in the community and have every opportunity for inclusion in other settings – attending college, work placements, etc. The other areas for extra provision are sensory rooms, which are age appropriate in each of the phases. There will also be soft play areas; withdrawal areas in each classroom; two-way windows for professionals and parents to observe their child; a hydrotherapy pool; flexible drama and performance areas, a café to be run by students in conjunction with the catering services; and horticulture areas to be run in conjunction with grounds maintenance services.

Three designs were submitted and the final one was decided by the local authority following the school's own evaluations.

arrangements require careful planning by both the special school and others as the example of Thomas Bewick School, Newcastle upon Tyne illustrates (see Box 1.2).

Dual registration

Given that a special and a mainstream school have developed an understanding of each other's provision, including their respective curricula and teaching methods, the dual registration of certain pupils with SEN becomes practicable. Careful consideration is given to the amount of time a particular pupil might spend in each setting, and what curriculum subjects are followed in each place of learning. Decisions might be made taking into account the strengths and weaknesses of each school in a variation of 'optimal education' (e.g. Farrell, 2005: 101–3). For example, if a particular special school has very limited facilities and resources for information and communication technology, it might be beneficial for some of its pupils to attend a better-equipped mainstream school for such lessons, all other things being equal.

Box 1.3 ASPLEY WOOD SCHOOL, NOTTINGHAM

Part-time placements in mainstream schools

Aspley Wood School, Nottingham (www.aspleywood.nottingham.sch.uk), is a co-educational community special school for 40 pupils with physical disabilities and complex learning difficulties. It has a British Council International School Award; a Schools Curriculum Award (2000 and 2002); a School Achievement Award (2003); a Sport for All Award; and has Investors in People recognition. As well as teachers and teaching assistants, the school has its own therapists and nurses and is visited by social workers, a music therapist and a teacher for the deaf. Outreach to mainstream schools educating pupils with physical disabilities includes helping the LEA allocate funds to mainstream schools for equipment or special seating.

Some Aspley School pupils have part-time placements in their local mainstream schools. To set up and maintain these placements requires careful collaboration between teachers, therapists, parents, teaching assistants and the pupils. Factors to be taken into account include: accessibility of mainstream premises; transport arrangements; the alignment of timetables; intimate personal care procedures in the mainstream setting; feeding requirements; friendship groups; moving and handling training; any specialised seating/tables required; access to the curriculum; and communication between all parties. There is ongoing monitoring and support of placements, which are regularly reviewed.

Staff from the special school may support the pupil in mainstream and provide opportunities for colleagues from the mainstream school to observe good practice in the special school and model suitable approaches. Communications between the two schools may be facilitated through a joint pupil diary. Where a special school has several pupils on dual role with different mainstream schools with teachers and other professionals from the special school involved, it is essential that communications are effective and well organised.

The child's statement of SEN would record the fact that the pupil has placements in two schools. Evaluating dual placements may involve monitoring and evaluating the progress of individual pupils according to where they were educated, for what subjects, for what amount of time and so on. An example of a school with long experience of dual registration and placement (Hexham Priory School, Northumberland) is given in Chapter 10.

The example of Aspley Wood School also illustrates some of the considerations to be taken into account (see Box 1.3).

Extended schools and children's centres

Evidence from the USA suggests that extending the time of the school day in mainstream schools does not necessarily lead to improvements in pupils' learning (Ellis, 1984). However, the extended school concept does not simply have to be limited to making the day longer but can involve making the time that the school operates more flexible and also 'extending' what the school does.

An extended school has been described as 'one that provides a range of services and activities often beyond the school day to help meet the needs of its pupils, their families and the wider community' (DfES, 2002: 2). Under the Education Act 2002, governing bodies can provide facilities and services benefiting families and the community; arrange with other partners to provide services on the school premises; and can charge for services (see also www. continyu.org.uk). The management of larger programmes might be delegated to, for example, early years development and childcare partnerships.

The current encouragement for the development of extended schools including so-called full service schools and children's centres have relevance for special schools in that there are already examples of special schools offering extended services. (See, for example, Box 1.4.) Any school considering such a development can begin by consulting the legal, practical and financial advice available on the Internet, for example at Teachernet (www.teachernet.gov.uk).

Extended schools are considered an important element in achieving Every Child Matters outcomes, providing as they do services and activities, often beyond the school day, for pupils and families and the community. A full-service school embracing principles of integrating children's services might offer:

- childcare (e.g. working with early years development childcare partnerships to plan childcare services, Sure Start, Early Excellence centres);
- study support;
- community sports programmes and cultural activities;
- family learning (e.g. family literacy and numeracy);
- adult education and lifelong learning (e.g. neighbourhood learning centres);
- health services (e.g. liaison with the primary care trust and others; family health centres);
- social care services; and
- access to school facilities such as information and communication technology.

An example of the potential for developing sports programmes is Physical Education, School Sport and Club Links (PESSCL), a government strategy aimed at increasing the number of children and young people aged 5 to 16 years who take up and enjoy sports within and beyond the curriculum. This

Box 1.4 HADRIAN SCHOOL, NEWCASTLE UPON TYNE

Hadrian School, Newcastle upon Tyne Is a community day school for 125 boys and girls aged 2 to 11 years with severe learning difficulties and profound and multiple learning difficulties and associated physical disabilities. The school has a wide range of partners including: Sport England, the School Sports Partnership, Northern Arts, Northern Stage, Friends of Hadrian School, Newcastle Business Partnership, Sightlines Initiative, Newcastle Toy Library, the University of Northumbria and various local schools and colleges.

The school runs an after-school club with a rolling programme of activities including: games; athletics and trampolining; hydrotherapy; cooking; information and communication technology; music; and art. The Newcastle Toy Library has a base in the school and hosts fortnightly activities on Saturday mornings including soft play and aromatherapy. The Play and Youth Service use the school every holiday period except Christmas for a play scheme for young people and children with SEN and their siblings. Local health authorities have staff based on the school site including physiotherapists and speech and language therapists. The LA employs and pays for an occupational therapist and a physiotherapist who work in the school part-time.

Trainees and students including nursing, teaching, BTEC and medical students use Hadrian as a training placement. The school is the venue for adult courses and workshops such as first aid and moving and handling. It delivers courses for teachers and others including moving and handling; rebound therapy (accredited and offered nationally) and National Vocational Qualifications for teaching assistants (accredited by the City and Guilds of London Institute).

In developing as an extended school, Hadrian liaised with the LA to identify gaps in services and set out to rectify them. Funds are gained from various sources, for example National Lottery funding. Goals were identified and included, extending the opportunities for accredited courses and widening after-school activities. Progress towards these goals is monitored in ongoing meetings. Among the challenges that arise are that the background work (including completing applications for funding) is considerable and there are some limitations of space in the school now it has extended its services. In 2006 an extended schools committee was set up comprising staff and governors and a representative from a local department store with which the school already had strong links.

involves collaboration between the School Sport Partnership, County Sports Partnerships and sports clubs accredited as meeting national minimum standards by the national governing bodies to which they are affiliated (www. teachernet.gov.uk/pe). Also involved with the PESSCL strategy is the Child Protection in Sport Unit involving a partnership between the National Society for the Prevention of Cruelty to Children and Sport England who have established national standards for safeguarding and protecting children in sport (www.thecspu.org.uk/). The Youth Sport Trust (www.youthsporttrust.org) also supports projects that sometimes involve special schools. The Bexley School Sport Partnership aimed to improve behaviour and social skills for pupils with SEN and six schools, including a special school, used adventure-based learning in a six-week module, which the special school involved considered worthwhile.

A further example of extended school provision is the development of study support, perhaps drawing on the advice of the LA study support coordinator. This involves learning activities outside normal lesson time that young people take part in voluntarily, such as homework/study clubs, outdoor activities and sport, creative arts, mentoring, community volunteering, particular interests (e.g. information and communications technology) and learning about learning (study skills and thinking skills). It is expected to improve attainment, attitudes to school and attendance. A publication, *The Essential Guide to the Impact of Study Support*, may be found on the Standards site (www.standards.dfes.gov.uk/).

Specialist special schools

A 'specialist schools programme' was extended from its original curriculum-related remit to involve an SEN specialism. After 12 special schools were involved in pilot developments, the programme was extended to 50 more special schools (Beatie, 2006). These schools specialise in one of the four areas of SEN covered by the *Special Educational Needs Code of Practice* (DfES, 2001a): cognition; behavioural, emotional and social difficulties; communication; or physical sensory. The schools are expected to 'share expertise and resources with partner schools, support services, multi disciplinary agencies and the wider community' (Beatie, 2006: 1, point 1).

In their plans these specialist special schools are expected to reflect in particular:

- Every Child Matters outcomes;
- the Children's Services 'agenda', Trusts, Centres, extended and full-service schools;
- new training programmes and arrangements within the children's workforce strategy and school workforce remodelling; and

- integrated inspection framework, joint area reviews and the new OfSTED framework.

The Specialist Schools and Academies Trust (www.ssatrust.org.uk) and the Youth Sports Trust (www.youthsportstrust.org) provide support.

Among the overall aims of the programme are to 'Raise attainment for all students within the SEN specialist strand, in literacy, numeracy and personal, social and health education and across the whole curriculum', as indicated on the website. Collaboration is important, for example involving schools, services and multi-disciplinary agencies. Before applying for SSS status, the schools are expected to have already reached certain minimum standards, for example having a record of effective outreach working with mainstream schools and the wider community; creative practice and the assessment of 'need' and curriculum development; and links with children's services and working partnerships. (It is noticeable, given the supposed valuing of special schools, that the emphasis of government is on outreach rather than inreach so that it appears fine to encourage pupils in special schools to spend more time in mainstream but not so good for pupils in mainstream schools to spend more time in special.)

The five-year leading-edge partnership programme (to 2007), offering funding via a lead school to use across a partnership to work locally on learning 'challenges', focuses on raising standards and tackling underachievement of particular ethnic minority groups and pupils from poor socio-economic backgrounds.

Federations including special schools

The term 'federations' may refer to partnerships, clusters and collaborative groupings of schools and mergers creating new schools. One aim of federations is to enable schools to build capacity jointly and coherently. A continuum of federation/collaboration arrangements is suggested (www.standards. dfes.gov.uk/federations/pdf/FederationsContinuum): a 'hard governance federation'; a 'soft governance federation'; a 'soft federation'; and an 'informal, loose federation'.

A hard governance federation involves a group of schools having a single governing body statutorily established using the federation regulations under the Education Act 2002 section 24. All the schools share common goals through protocols and service-level agreements.

In a soft governance federation, each school has its own governing body but the federation has a joint governance/strategic committee with delegated powers statutorily established using collaboration regulations under the Education Act 2002 section 26. The schools share common goals through service-level agreements and protocols and the joint committee can make decisions in *some* areas.

A soft federation is a non-statutory arrangement in which each school has its own governing body, but the federation has a joint governance/strategic committee *without* delegated powers. All the schools share common goals through protocols and the joint committee can make joint *recommendations*.

In an informal, loose federation, which is non-statutory, each school has its own governing body and the group of schools meet informally, share common goals and can work together with informal arrangements. While the previous three forms of federation involve common management positions, an informal, loose collaboration is unlikely to do so.

Generic special schools

Having considered approaches to organisation and structure that a special school can develop in collaboration with other schools and with the local authority, I turn now to organisational issues surrounding the development of generic special schools. These educate pupils with different types of SEN such as moderate learning difficulties (MLD), severe learning difficulties (SLD), profound and multiple learning difficulties (PMLD) and autistic spectrum disorder (ASD) in the same school.

An important factor is how the school is organised to function at its best for all its pupils, whose range of prior attainment may be widely different. It may be helpful to remind readers of levels of attainment typical of pupils with MLD, SLD and PMLD, described in the government guidance on data collection entitled *Data Collection by Type of Special Educational Needs* (DfES, 2003a).

A pupil with MLD will be considerably behind other children of the same age who do not have an SEN. The child will have made slow progress leading to lower than average attainments. Accordingly, the description of pupils with MLD in the guidance (DfES, 2003a) includes that these pupils 'will have attainments considerably below expected levels in most areas of the curriculum, despite appropriate interventions' (ibid.: 3).

Regarding pupils with SLD, the guidance states that 'their attainments may be within the upper P range (P4 to P8) for much of their school careers (that is, below level 1 of the National Curriculum)' (ibid.: 3). To remind readers of the levels indicated in this description, the P levels for speaking and listening may provide an example. Level P4 is:

> Pupils repeat, copy and imitate between 10 and 20 single words, signs or phrases or use a repertoire of objects of reference or symbols. They use single words, signs and symbols for familiar objects, *for example, cup, biscuit*, and to communicate about events and feelings, *for example, likes and dislikes*. They respond appropriately to simple requests which contain one key word, sign or symbol in familiar situations, *for example, Get your*

coat, Stand up, or *Clap your hands.* They show an understanding of familiar objects.

> (QCA, 2001a: 30, italics in original to indicate examples
> particular to speaking and listening)

The description for P8 for speaking and listening is:

> Pupils link up to four key words, signs or symbols in communicating about their own experiences or in telling familiar stories, both in groups and one to one, for example, *'The hairy giant shouted at Finn'.* They use a growing vocabulary to convey meaning to the listener. They take part in role-play with confidence. They listen attentively. They follow requests and instructions with four key words, signs and symbols, *for example, 'Get the big book about dinosaurs from the library'.*
>
> (QCA, 2001a: 31)

Turning to pupils with PMLD, the guidance says, 'Their attainments are likely to remain in the early P scale range (P1 to 4) throughout their school careers (that is below level 1 of the National Curriculum)' (DfES, 2003a: 4). As readers may already be aware, the earlier levels of the P scales are the same from P level P1 to P3 for all subjects such as science, English and mathematics. Each is further subdivided into P1 (i), P1 (ii), P2 (i), P2 (ii), P3 (i) and P3 (ii).

P1 is: 'Pupils encounter activities and experiences. They may be passive or resistant. They may show simple reflex responses, *for example, startling at sudden noises or movements.* Any participation is fully prompted' (QCA, 2001a: 29, italics in original). An example of a P4 level (for science) is as follows:

> Pupils explore objects and materials provided, changing some materials by physical means and observing the outcomes, *for example, when mixing flour and water.* They know that certain actions produce predictable results, *for example that sponges can be squeezed.* Pupils communicate their awareness of changes in light, sound and movement. They imitate actions involving main body parts, *for example clapping or stamping.* They make sounds using their own body parts, *for example, tapping, singing or vocalising,* and imitate or copy sounds. They cause movement by a pushing or pulling action. Pupils show interest in wide range of living things, handling and observing them, *for example, on a visit to a farm, or on a walk into the woods collecting items.*
>
> (QCA, 2001b: 30, italics in original)

If special schools are necessary and important as schools in their own right, it is partly because of the difficulty a typical mainstream school has in educating pupils with very wide differences in their attainment. Such a difference may be found for example between a pupil achieving typically for his age and a pupil with MLD having 'attainments considerably below expected levels in most areas of the curriculum, despite appropriate interventions' (DfES, 2003a: 3). Given this, can it be expected that a special school educates effectively in the same groups pupils whose attainments may differ even more widely, for example pupils with MLD and pupils with SLD, or pupils with SLD and PMLD?

For some pupils with SLD, their attainments may overlap with those of a pupil with PMLD and the school may have a fairly easy decision that the

---

Box 1.5 ST HUGH'S SCHOOL, NORTH LINCOLNSHIRE

St Hugh's School, North Lincolnshire is a co-educational community 'generic' special school for 110 pupils aged 11 to 19 years having moderate learning difficulties (MLD), severe learning difficulties (SLD) or profound and multiple learning difficulties (PMLD), with some pupils having autistic spectrum disorder (ASD).

Core subjects of the curriculum are English; mathematics; science; information and communication technology; religious education; physical education; and personal, social, health and citizenship education. At Key Stage 3, the curriculum includes geography, history, music, art, French, and design and technology with most subjects being taught by specialist teachers. At Key Stage 4, history and geography are not taught to make room for transition-related areas of the curriculum. Careers education is taught as part of the preparation for adult life programme from year 9. The Key Stage 4 programme covers self-awareness, decision-making skills, and opportunity awareness and transition skills. Accreditation includes GCSEs, the AQA Unit Award Scheme and St John Ambulance Awards.

The school takes the view that inclusion can take place within a special school when pupils with different SEN are educated together, but this is an evidence-based view. Where differences in different pupils' prior learning is so wide that it is considered to inhibit academic and personal progress to educate them together, the school has resource bases where groups of pupils can be better educated separately as necessary. There is such a resource base for pupils with PMLD and for pupils with ASD. There are also two classrooms for pupils with PMLD aged over 16 years for whom local colleges cannot suitably provide.

pupils will make good progress in the same groupings. But for most pupils there are wide differences in levels of attainment. The generic special school has to decide on its groupings of pupils, and may decide that pupils with MLD, SLD and PMLD will make better progress if taught predominantly or partially separately. This may be for all subjects and areas of the curriculum or for certain ones such as literacy and numeracy.

Flexible grouping may be used and the special school may wish to monitor their impact. Such arrangements might be informed by the principles of optimal education (Farrell, 2006f: 14–25), that is, groupings could be informed by the rate of progress that pupils make in 'academic' areas and in personal and social development.

As can be seen from the example of St Hugh's School (see Box 1.5), one way of organising for pupils with different SEN is to have a resource base and for some pupils discrete classrooms. Other ways are to have 'sets' throughout the school, for example for pupils with MLD, SLD and PMLD in English and mathematics and perhaps other arrangements for other subjects, some being set while others mix pupils with MLD, SLD and PMLD.

The special school as a coherent educational provision

Given the potential for changing and extending the structure and organisation of the special school in so many ways, it is important to keep its focus as a coherent educational provision in its own right clearly in mind. Tension arises, for example, in creating dual registration/placement structures involving outreach services where special school staff, including teachers, may spend a considerable amount of time in mainstream schools supporting pupils and where there may be concerns that this will lead to a lowering of the quality of education for pupils taught mainly or solely in the special school. This leads into the topic of the next chapter, which considers outreach and other roles of the special school.

Thinking points

Readers may wish to consider:

- how priorities for particular forms of organisation and structures are determined;
- how the effectiveness of the special school in optimising its structures is to be monitored and evaluated;
- if the generic special school is to have flexibility to educate some pupils with different SEN for some of the time in different groups, the architectural, financial and staffing implications involved.

Key text

Farrell, M. (2006) *Celebrating the Special School*, London, David Fulton Publishers.

Chapter 2 of the above book outlines weaknesses in that aspect of inclusion advocating fewer pupils with SEN in special schools and more in mainstream schools. It considers social views of SEN, moral claims for inclusion and empirical evidence. The book explains in detail the approach of optimal education in which the venue for a child's education is informed by his educational progress and personal, emotional and social development.

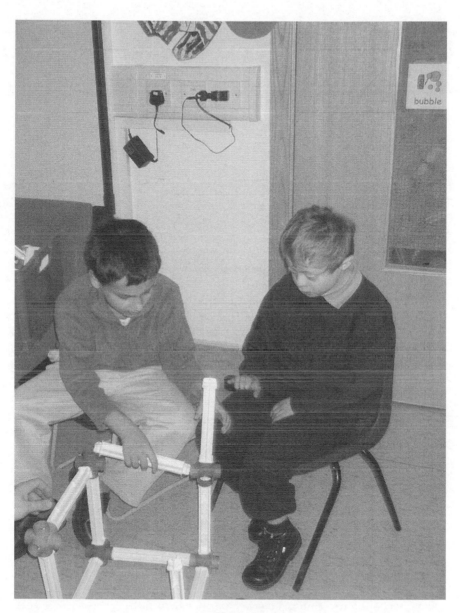

Building frame

Chapter 2

Clear roles

This chapter looks at the role of special schools in providing outreach, inreach, and training and consultancy. It examines ways in which special schools support mainstream schools in educating a wider range of pupils with SEN than they might presently. Next, the chapter looks more specifically at inreach and outreach. I then consider special schools offering training and consultancy, including in the area of curriculum development to others. Within this context, I look at the relationship between local authorities and independent and non-maintained special schools.

Throughout, the chapter argues, in line with the approach of 'optimal education' (Farrell, 2006f: ch. 2), for the equal importance of outreach and inreach so that both are informed by the academic progress and personal development that pupils make, as the main determiner of whether pupils are predominantly educated in special or mainstream schools or the proportion of time a pupil is educated in either.

Special schools supporting mainstream schools

Clearly, there are links between the structure and organisation of the special school considered in the previous chapter, and the four roles of outreach, inreach, training and consultancy. Where pupils are collocated or where pupils are dually registered, there are opportunities and implications for all four roles.

Although one role for special schools is that of supporting mainstream schools in educating a wider range of pupils with SEN than they might at present, this does not necessarily imply that the numbers of pupils in special schools will reduce as a result.

For example, an increasing number of pupils considered to have SEN may be identified in mainstream schools that may not in any event have attended special school. These pupils may be considered to have types of SEN that are difficult to identify and define, for example developmental coordination disorder/dyspraxia; dyslexia; dyscalculia; behavioural, emotional and social difficuilties; or autistic spectrum disorder. Or a special school for pupils with behavioural, emotional and social difficulties may support a mainstream school enabling it to educate pupils with behaviourial, emotional and social difficulties (BESD) who might otherwise attend a local pupil referral unit either part-time or full-time.

To take another example, consider a special school designated for pupils with MLD whose pupils also experience additional difficulties such as speech and language difficulties and BESD. This school may well be educating increasing numbers of pupils with MLD and these additional difficulties. But at the same time, it might be working to enable a mainstream school to educate newly referred pupils with MLD who did not also have additional difficulties. The numbers of pupils with particular types of SEN appear to be increasing, for example pupils with medical conditions leading to SEN. In such instances, the special school can assist a mainstream school to provide for some pupils whose medical needs are less complex.

Where special schools and mainstream schools work together in this way, there is some overlap with outreach, and with developing mainstream staff members' skills and understanding through training and consultancy. These are considered later. A precursor to effective approaches is that special and mainstream schools develop shared values and a shared understanding of the aims of the support. Both of these take time and effort to develop. As a starting point, the then Teacher Training Agency standards can be used in relation to a special school developing staff for advisory roles and responsibilities (Teacher Training Agency, 1999: 278).

Outreach

If outreach is taken to mean the work of special schools in reaching out to others especially mainstream schools, to help them better educate pupils with SEN, various approaches come under its remit.

The document *Inclusion: The Impact of LEA Support and Outreach Services* (OfSTED, 2005c) gives a useful indication of some of the issues for special schools concerning outreach. The report reviewed the quality of external SEN support for schools analysing good practice based on inspection visits to six LEAs and reports of inspections of schools and LEAs in the years 2003 and 2004. Its main focus was LEA support services and outreach services from special schools. The report indicates that generic standards proposed by the Department for Education and Skills could form a basis for improving external services, indeed an annex to the report comprises a contribution to developing these.

The South West SEN Regional Partnership publication (Newport, 2004) offers helpful examples of outreach and a self-evaluation sheet for providers (South West SEN Regional Partnership, 2004). Other examples are also to be found (see Box 2.1).

> ## Box 2.1 EXAMPLES OF SPECIAL SCHOOL OUTREACH
>
> A special schoolteacher trainer visits a mainstream primary school for ten weekly sessions to work with a teacher, a teaching assistant and a group of six to eight pupils having difficulties with social communication. They draw on the 'Social Use of Language Programme' (Rinaldi, 1992/2001), which seeks to teach and encourage better communication skills. The members of staff observe and prepare to use the approach later with other small groups, initially with the special school teacher's support and guidance.
>
> A boarding special school offers a fixed-term placement for pupils with behavioural, emotional and social difficulties with outreach structures intended to help the pupil to return to mainstream school within an agreed time. The support includes special school staff visiting the proposed mainstream school to ensure mainstream staff are aware of the particular difficulties of the pupil, have strategies to respond to them, and are aware that they can later make contact with the special school for advice. The special school programme is geared from the start to the gradual return of the pupil to mainstream.
>
> A special schoolteacher works with colleagues in a mainstream school to develop and assess a new intervention, for example a scheme for teaching reading to pupils with dyslexia. The special schoolteacher acts as an independent evaluator of the intervention.
>
> Staff in a special school provide speech and language assessments for pupils educated in a mainstream school.
>
> The special school provides advice about and creates resources for a mainstream school, for example in relation to a pupil with visual impairment.

A special school considering developing outreach services may wish to explain their proposals to other special schools so there is no divisive competition, and to local mainstream schools to ensure there is a need for what is to be offered. Mainstream schools that are serious about using the proposed service may put in writing their support and negotiate with the local authority and others about how the service is to be funded. Also, in early liaison with the LA, the special schools may wish to ensure that they speak with one voice, making the cost of providing outreach clear. Formal agreements about the outreach service can be linked to the LA's overall strategy.

Among other features that tend to facilitate effective outreach are that protocols are agreed in advance, for example between the schools involved and any LA staff such as an educational psychologist who might also have a role. A business plan, perhaps extending for five years, can help structure the service and would include costs, quality criteria and time schedules. Looking

Box 2.2 THOMAS WOLSEY SCHOOL, SUFFOLK

Thomas Wolsey School, Ipswich, Suffolk is a community school for 82 pupils aged 3 to 19 years with complex physical and sensory impairments, some of whom also have other learning difficulties. Around 50 per cent of pupils have no verbal language and use alternative and augmentative communication systems.

The outreach service at the school began in the year 2000 in response to requests from some parents for their child to spend some time in mainstream school. Initially, Thomas Wolsey was unsure whether mainstream colleagues would be able to provide education of the right quality and it therefore developed a support system offering advice and training.

The school started with a budget allocation of £50,000 enabling it to appoint an outreach manager and train a member of the existing support team as a manual-handling trainer. Thomas Wolsey set up a steering group including representatives of LEA officers and advisory teachers (for learning support and therapy teams) to monitor the development of the service and to evaluate outcomes. The group continues to meet termly, supporting the development of the service and providing the LEA with evaluations of the performance of the service and the levels of demand.

Among the difficulties faced in seeking to place pupils in mainstream schools is that mainstream teachers may lack knowledge about the particular impact of disabilities on access to learning, medical needs, the pupil's ability to access the curriculum for physical education, the differentiation required, manual handling and risk assessment; all of which special school staff build up over many years. Thomas Wolsey has therefore placed emphasis on the transition process, working with mainstream colleagues, sharing information about individual pupils, ensuring access issues are tackled, and that manual-handling procedures are known and risk assessments are made prior to the pupil attending mainstream school.

Thomas Wolsey staff continue to attend the pupil's annual reviews of statements throughout the pupil's placement in mainstream and the school offers training and support at times of transitions, for example to a new class, a new Key Stage, or for transfer from primary to secondary phase.

The school also organises focus days for pupils with different lower incidence disabilities such as hemiplegia, Duchenne muscular dystrophy or epilepsy. These include parents and the pupil's classroom assistant and the day is programmed to offer the pupils opportunities to access specialist physical education, information and communication technology, and social activities while the parents have the opportunity to meet and get to know each other. Parents have specifically positively evaluated these days.

From January 2005, a specialist assessment centre has been based at the school for assessing children's ability to access computer or communication aids and environmental control devices.

For some pupils, outreach has led to them having a dual placement with a mainstream school and Thomas Wolsey. In 2006, there were 29 pupils on dual placements, supported by the outreach service. Monitoring and evaluation of pupils' progress is an essential part of the service, with termly reviews of individual education plans and targets for each pupil. Additionally, the school continues to offer a similar service for pupils who have transferred to a full-time placement, especially at transfer and transition stages.

Box 2.3 MELDRETH MANOR SCHOOL, HERTFORDSHIRE

Meldreth Manor School, Royston, Hertfordshire (www.meldrethmanor.org.uk) is an independent co-educational boarding special school educating about 30 pupils aged 8 to 19 years with cerebral palsy and profound and multiple learning difficulties. It is one of the special educational needs schools supported by the charity Scope (www.scope.org.uk).

Meldreth Manor offers outreach services under the title 'Creating Connections'. This is an inclusive service focusing on working with staff and resources to support the development of inclusive education for students with disabilities. Outreach services are provided for children and adults needing a multi-sensory approach and/or augmentative and alternative approach to communication, education or leisure and for the professionals who support them. This offers a multi-disciplinary assessment relating to multiple disability and visual impairment (MDVI); augmentative and alternative communication; and information and communication technology and involves a range of professionals including speech and language therapists, physiotherapists and other professionals to a range of establishments.

Creating Connections provides courses that, depending on their content, are intended for parents; staff in special schools and mainstream schools including teachers and teaching assistants; and others. Examples include: 'Supporting communication through alternative and augmentative communication', 'Teaching multi-sensory drama', 'Introduction to Makaton', 'Making sense of multi-sensory approaches for the curriculum' and 'Developing switch skills'.

The school website provides details of current courses.

beyond that timescale, the school and others involved will want to ensure the longer term continuation and success of the service. What exactly is to be offered would be clearly specified. Built into the plan would be arrangements for the evaluation of the service.

I suggest that, in line with the approach of 'optimal education' (Farrell, 2006f: ch. 2), outreach can be usefully informed and guided by its impact on the academic progress and personal development of pupils, so that if the service leads to lower standards for pupils with SEN in the special school or in the mainstream school, it is reviewed.

Funding, which needs to be clear from the start, may include: LA funding, sponsorship, pro rata charges to mainstream schools, top slicing mainstream school funding, funding extra unfilled pupil places for special schools, quid pro quo arrangements and money from charitable trusts.

It follows from what has already been said that among the factors that can get in the way of effective outreach are ad hoc approaches, piecemeal funding and tension between the responsibilities of a special school to its pupils and its outreach commitments. To some degree such difficulties can be forestalled by careful market research and market priming, long-term planning, starting small, involving the LA and others at an early stage, ensuring co-operation not competition, and developing clear service-level agreements between schools and other agencies for pupils and their families. (See, for example, Box 2.2)

Outreach may also be offered of course by non-maintained or independent special schools, as the services offered by Meldreth Manor School illustrate (see Box 2.3).

Inreach

Some examples of inreach are described below (see Box 2.4).

For the purposes of the present section, I propose that inreach be taken to refer mainly to special schools bringing into the school pupils from mainstream schools and elsewhere to contribute to their better education and development.

In the document *Inclusion: The Impact of LEA Support and Outreach Services* (OfSTED, 2005c) mentioned earlier, it was noted, 'Special schools were unclear whether the provision for outreach services was intended to help schools include more effectively the pupils already based in mainstream schools, or whether the intention was to reduce the number of pupils in special schools' (ibid.: para. 20). The report continues:

> For example, in one special school an outreach teacher was working with four pupils from a mainstream school who were taught at the special school for one morning a week. By the end of the term, two of the four pupils were placed full time in the special school. This example reflects the view that the provision of outreach services can be a way of securing the survival of special schools.
>
> (ibid.: para. 21)

Box 2.4 EXAMPLES OF SPECIAL SCHOOL INREACH

In a special school for pupils with behavioural, emotional and social difficulties, as a form of early intervention, emotional literacy group sessions are offered to local mainstream schools.

Groups of pupils are transported to the special school for morning or afternoon sessions perhaps once a week. The special school provides eight sessions per week over four days and the special school staff use the remaining day for administration, school visits and so on.

A residential special school provides a day nursery on its premises for local children.

Teachers from a mainstream school make structured visits to a special school to observe lessons, discuss approaches with staff and study resources. A special school teacher visits them in their mainstream school to observe them trying new approaches and advises and supports them.

It is important to remember that the OfSTED report (2005c) is focused on the provision of outreach, not on the potential parallel activity of inreach. Also, it is not possible to comment on the example above, not knowing the facts of the particular case. But the observations mentioned in the previous paragraph raise important points.

Where a teacher who is working on outreach is in fact developing inreach, this may be confusing, even (if funding is specifically for outreach) inappropriate. However, if the relationship between special schools and mainstream schools were based on optimising the progress of pupils educationally and in terms of social and personal development in line with 'optimal education' (Farrell, 2006f: ch. 2), there would be nothing inappropriate in pupils moving from mainstream to special schools where lack of progress in a mainstream school suggested it. In other words, outreach and inreach would have equal value. (See, for example, Box 2.5.)

Training and consultancy

Considerations when a special school proposes offering training to others include determining:

- the best venue (LA offices, the special school, a mainstream school that is buying in the training);

Box 2.5 SPRINGFIELDS SCHOOL, WILTSHIRE

Springfields School, Wiltshire is a Specialist Sports College and Vocational Training Centre with residential accommodation and educates 68 secondary-age pupils having social, emotional and behavioural difficulties. The school provides tuition in externally accredited vocational subjects to 400 pupils from another 17 mainstream and special schools and has an emotional literacy centre (the SpEL Centre) attended part-time by Key Stage 1 and 2 pupils. The school ethos is based on cognitive behavioural therapy enabling pupils to recognise the causes and triggers of behaviour and how to react more productively and acceptably in society.

As a specialist college, the school chose sport as its specialism and information technology as a second subject, to help ensure all students have an appropriate kinaesthetic-based curriculum. As a Sports College, Springfields has improved collaboration with other agencies, and its sharing of good practice, information and resources as well as developing staff expertise. The school provides children, families and other members of the community access to sporting and educational services, building on well-established multi-agency working practices.

Springfields offers the following five vocational courses – motor vehicles, construction, catering, sport and horticulture. Up to 17 schools and YPSS (Young People's Support Service) centres use these facilities and nearly 400 pupils attend per week. Qualified assessors teach the courses and all courses are unit-based. All assessments are verified both internally and externally. For many pupils in Springfields' curriculum-partnership schools this is an opportunity to show what they can achieve in a slightly different setting and for some it is the first time they have been successful in anything.

The SpEL Centre is a specialist primary setting providing short-term, targeted intervention focusing on the development of appropriate social, behavioural and learning skills with vulnerable children, their schools and families. The programme is facilitated through an emotional literacy curriculum underpinned by positive behaviour management. The work with parents developing their skills, and with schools promoting inclusive practices, is a key feature of a successful outcome for the children. The school opened a second Centre in Trowbridge in 2006.

- the most effective resources (computer presentations, hand outs, discussion groups, DVD, audio tapes, follow up access to the school's Internet site, follow up telephone or e-mail contact to reinforce practical applications); and
- the time of the training (day, in-service training day, twilight).

Among training that can be provided by a special school are the examples shown in Box 2.6.

Box 2.6 EXAMPLES OF SPECIAL SCHOOL TRAINING

Training for staff in a mainstream school in the use of new resources, the use of finely graded assessments and their moderation (P scales, B Squared, PIVATS), systems of assessment and monitoring using information and communications technology, advice and information about a particular type of SEN and suitable approaches.

Training for parents, such as workshops and training in particular approaches, such as behaviour management or reading. Early intervention training may include the special school providing a crèche for children for the first part of a session then having the child and parents come together to try the approaches.

Training for governors of mainstream schools having a particular interest in SEN (all governors have responsibility for SEN).

A course for parents and professionals launching a new curriculum or assessment procedures.

Training and information sharing for LEA officers to demonstrate the special school's successes.

Objectives can be agreed in advance with evaluations of the training relating to the extent to which the objectives were achieved so that the special school has information that helps it improve the service.

Consultancy might include:

- mentoring a mainstream school SEN coordinator through a period of change;
- long-term support for staff setting up a unit in a mainstream school; and
- providing a 'hot line' for advice funded by a retainer fee and where calls are logged and charged.

Box 2.7 CUCKMERE HOUSE SCHOOL, EAST SUSSEX

Cuckmere House School, Seaford, East Sussex is an LEA-maintained day school with a boarding facility, for 64 boys resident in East Sussex and aged 5 to 16 years with severe behavioural, emotional and social difficulties. The school was designated as a Trailblazer Specialist SEN college in 2005 and is also part of a federation of schools. Cuckmere House is part of 'Behaviour Support Service West' offering support to the western half of East Sussex. The roles of the school and the services it offers are diverse.

In the primary phase, the school provides full-time placement at the school for pupils with a statement for BESD. It has a primary outreach programme involving a team of teaching assistants who work half the week in Cuckmere House and the other half in ordinary primary schools. It manages a junior pupil referral unit with places for eight full-time pupils or the part-time equivalent. Cuckmere House is one of ten lead behaviour schools in the county, developing and disseminating best practice in behavioural management across the county and is introducing Social Emotional Aspects of Learning (SEAL) within the curriculum.

At secondary level, the school provides full-time places for boys with a statement of BESD and a specialist unit for vulnerable boys unable to access the facilities at Key Stage 4 (14 to 16 years). There is a transition project with local schools to support pupils considered at risk of exclusion. As part of the federation of schools within East Sussex, Cuckmere House provides training and consultancy to mainstream schools.

Through the behaviour support service the school manages two pupil referral units for secondary-phase pupils including providing a young women's support worker, and provides a behaviour support team comprising teachers and teaching assistants including a specialist infant support teacher. It manages a work placement team, the educational aspect of a secure unit and an area reintegration officer team.

Cuckmere House also developed continuing professional development for support staff; piloted a national programme for specialist leaders of behaviour and attendance; begun working with Brighton University to contribute to teacher training; and has started to develop a resource centre on behaviour for schools. This will eventually provide schools with a lending service for materials, literature and video/DVD as well as a training centre and an advice clinic through video conferencing.

A member of special school staff may draw on counselling skills. For example, in some instances direct advice may not be needed but a reflective exploration of the issues might be more effective, enabling the 'consultee' to evaluate and decide options themselves (see Box 2.7 on p.25).

Relationships between LAs and non-maintained and independent special schools

Independent or non-maintained special schools are more likely to offer boarding facilities than are LA-maintained special schools. This allows them to offer regional or national services but raises challenges in terms of contact with the pupils' families and general contact with the pupils' home localities.

Where LEAs interpret inclusion as indicating that pupils should be taught in their own locality including in local special schools, this can make LA officers less enthusiastic about placing pupils a long way away from home. Not only is such a placement likely to be expensive, it may be harder for the LA as well as the family to keep contacts with the school where it is a considerable distance away. The benefits have to be perceived as considerable. For example, home circumstances may be very fraught and a boarding provision may be seen as providing the round the clock support that is necessary. Also, the boarding school may have strategies to aid the child's transfer to his own locality in a specified time. Chelfham Mill School (www.chelfham millschool.co.uk) for boys with BESD has such a strategy for some of its pupils.

Despite some differences, a great deal of the work carried out by maintained, non-maintained and independent special schools is similar. Where the three types of school liaise in a particular locality (which may coincide with an LA boundary or that of two or three LAs) benefits can arise. The LA's strategic vision of provision can include that made by independent and non-maintained schools, for example by ensuring that there are a range of special schools educating pupils with different main types of SEN in their locality so parents have a choice of special school for different types of SEN.

Independent and non-maintained schools also offer services to the community and local mainstream schools. For example, the National Institute of Conductive Education, Birmingham, an independent school, is a training centre for student 'conductors' offering degree-level training, plus outreach services including sessional services for conditions such as dyspraxia, early intervention for children aged three to seven years, consultancy and staff training (www.conductiveeducation.org.uk).

Thinking points

Readers may wish to consider in the case of a particular special school:

• the balance of outreach and inreach and the values underpinning each;
• the balance between offering effective services for others and maintaining high standards for the pupils predominantly educated in the special school.

Key resources

Newport, F. (2004) *Outreach Support from Special Schools*, Taunton, South West SEN Regional Partnership (see also www.sw-special.co.uk/).

This document provides examples of outreach and is complemented by the South West SEN Regional Partnership *Self Evaluation Framework for Outreach Providers*, published in Taunton in 2004.

The above document was followed by South West SEN Regional Partnership *Effective Outreach for Special Schools: A Practical Handbook* in 2006. This is for special schools in the maintained or non-maintained sector who wish to start or develop outreach.

Office for Standards in Education (2005c) *Inclusion: The Impact of LEA Support and Outreach Services*, London, OfSTED.

This report indicates some of the issues for special schools concerning outreach.

Castle

Chapter 3

Challenging training

Introduction

Much is said and written about special schools sharing their expertise with mainstream schools, parents and others but the question of how special schools themselves ensure that their staff maintain and develop up-to-date skills and understanding seems to attract less attention. Yet it is crucial that special school staff are at the forefront of thought and action in educating pupils with SEN. Also, a range of high quality training and professional development can act as an encouragement in recruiting and retaining staff at all levels.

In this chapter, I remind readers of the background to workforce reform and remodelling in England with some of its implications for the continuing training and professional development of a range of staff. In this context, I look particularly at the changing roles of teaching assistants and higher level teaching assistants and at the work of school midday supervisory assistants and transport assistants/escorts.

Turning to teachers, the chapter outlines some of the courses offered mainly for experienced special school teachers and others by universities, local authorities, private companies and charitable bodies. I then look at courses run mainly by special schools themselves. (These courses do not occupy watertight compartments, for example a university and an LA may work together to run a programme.) Finally, the chapter touches on ways a special school can coordinate training to benefit the school and its pupils.

Workforce reform

When, in January 2003, local employers, school workforce unions and the Department for Education and Skills signed a national agreement on workforce reforms it was hoped to reduce teachers' overall hours through, for example, ensuring that head teachers and teachers do not routinely carry out administrative and clerical tasks; and reduce unnecessary paperwork and bureaucracy (e.g. DfES, 2003b: 7–8). Necessary changes in teachers' conditions of service were implemented between 2003 and 2006.

All teachers in maintained schools employed under the School Teachers Pay and Conditions Document were guaranteed a minimum of 10 per cent of timetabled teaching time as planning, preparation and assessment (PPA) from September 2005 to be used for individual or collaborative professional activity. Related to this was a programme of change management aimed at helping schools to implement the modifications to contracts and address the aims of the agreement.

In support of this, the Training and Development Agency for Schools (TDA) provided guidance to schools on good practice in implementing changes in teachers' contracts, and its website (www.tda.gov.uk) explained various strategies (inevitably called 'tools') such as brainstorming and a strengths, weaknesses, opportunities, threats (SWOT) analysis. A 'remodelling' process was advocated intended to enable schools and their partners to identify and agree where change was necessary and collaborate with others including other schools. Each LEA had a remodelling adviser who coordinated remodelling training for schools and, in some areas, remodelling steering groups were formed.

It was suggested (National Remodelling Team, 2004) (www.remodelling. org) that schools could free up PPA time by remodelling the workforce and implement PPA by strategies such as maximising the existing teaching resources and timetabling additional resources.

Teaching assistants and other support staff

Among staff roles that are continuing to develop after the stimulus of work-force reform are those of teaching assistants and higher level teaching assistants. This section also looks at the important roles of school midday supervisory assistants and transport assistants/escorts.

Training and teaching assistants

As already indicated, among aspects of remodelling is the development and flexibility of the teaching assistant's role. Flexible organisation might allow two or three TAs not to be allocated to a particular class but to be able to help with a specified lesson or with a certain pupil. Some TAs may be given extra training to specialise in a subject area and be allocated to support these lessons across the school, organising resources and providing more focused support. Or they may take extra training in a skill such as manual signing and teach it across the school to teachers and other TAs. Also, TAs are used in some schools to cover for absent teachers on their first day of absence. In supporting planning, preparation and assessment, TAs may work in pairs in classrooms while the teacher undertakes PPA work, perhaps with a named teacher on call if needed.

To sustain these roles, the school may provide regular training and support, for example inviting all TAs to in-service training days (and paying them

Box 3.1 CROSSHILL SCHOOL, BLACKBURN

Crosshill School, Blackburn, Lancashire is an LEA community co-educational special school for 108 pupils aged 11 to 16 years having moderate learning difficulties. It has strong links with ordinary schools and was the first special school in England to gain phase 2 specialist technology college status.

Crosshill has been developing staff training, including training days and twilight sessions, for over a decade and the training allows the use of a model that encourages flexibility in deploying staff and advantages for the pupils. All staff including teaching assistants and other support staff attend training and curriculum development sessions after school once a week for one and a half hours. Several support staff have taken degree courses and moved on to qualified teacher status and in the year 2006–7 six staff are studying for degrees. A popular option for support staff is to have a part-time teacher role paid as an unqualified teacher for part of their contract and to be employed as a teaching assistant for the rest of their contract.

The proportion of the contract for each role can vary according to the requirements of the school and the member of staff concerned. For example, a support assistant with an education degree specialising in art spends 60 per cent of the time as an unqualified teacher teaching art to all pupils aged 11 to 14 years and General Certificate in Education courses to groups of students aged 14 to 16 years, with the remainder of the time spent working as a support member of staff. Another staff member with an accountancy degree teaches business studies to three small groups of pupils aged 14 to 16 years for 30 per cent of the time, spending the remainder as a support teacher. A support assistant with a degree in information and communication technology teaches for 40 per cent of the time with the remainder spent gathering and analysing summative assessment data and providing some in-class support.

Staff appreciate having the opportunity to teach without the full responsibilities of full-time teaching. The school ensures that support staff are fully aware of the curriculum content, assessment and the course for pupils aged 14 to 16 years. Consequently, the school has not had to employ a supply teacher for some years. The teacher's role has changed to include that of facilitator, trainer and mentor. This model is supported by wide-ranging training. It has been found to provide wider curriculum options for students and ensures smaller teaching groups.

overtime); providing mentoring and monitoring, setting up appraisal meetings and reviews; and arranging regular group meetings to discuss issues. Job descriptions may be modified and updated as necessary and new protocols devised. (See, for example, Box 3.1 on p. 31.)

Training and higher level teaching assistants

The Training and Development Agency for Schools (TDA) *Professional Standards for Higher Level Teaching Assistants* (www.tda.gov.uk/support/hlta/ professstandards) cover the interrelated areas of professional values and practice; knowledge and understanding; and teaching and learning activities (TDA, 2006a). Supporting these standards are a *Handbook for Candidates* (TDA, 2006b); a *Handbook for Providers of Preparation and Assessment* (TDA, 2006c); and *Guidance on the Standards* (TDA, 2006d).

A framework of training, preparation and assessment has been developed. Steps for achieving higher level teaching assistant (HLTA) status (see e.g. TDA, 2006b: 27) comprise: getting the approval of the head teacher or line manager; applying to the local authority for funding and receiving confirmation of this; undergoing a training needs assessment carried out by the local authority or school to determine whether any training is needed to reach the standards (and completing any training necessary); attending a preparation for assessment course; having an assessment involving a school visit from a 'regional provider of assessment' (there is one for each Government Office region); and receiving an HLTA outcome letter.

Training is offered locally either from schools, local authorities or independent training providers. Candidates not eligible for TDA funding via their local authority because they work in a *non*-maintained school can fund themselves or apply to their school for funding and then apply directly to a regional assessment provider for the HLTA programme (www.tda.gov.uk/ support/hlta/becomingahlta/funding).

Supporting school midday supervisory assistants and transport assistants/escorts

School midday supervisory assistants and transport assistants/escorts are not particularly well paid but their role is important to the safety and well-being of pupils. It may be difficult for the special school to motivate, support and show that it values such staff.

One way of the special school demonstrating that it values these staff members is to ensure that there are well-developed systems for inducting them. For example, a midday supervisory assistant may be given an induction day before starting work that might include elements such as ensuring that they:

- are aware of child safety procedures and know who to go to if there is a concern;
- have visited all the classrooms and met teachers and other staff;
- are aware of the layout of the school and its grounds and of any areas that might require particular vigilance; and
- know the school routines leading up to and following on from the mid day session.

Another way to demonstrate that the school values these staff, which is also important in its own right, is to ensure that there is time for an effective handover of duties. In the morning and in the afternoon, time can be allocated and arrangements made so that escorts and teachers can exchange information and notes or diaries to aid communication with the home. Before lunchtimes teachers can inform school midday supervisory assistants of anything that has happened in the morning that could have a bearing on the smooth running of lunchtime. After lunch break, SMSAs can pass on information about what has happened to teachers and others. This often requires no more than that teachers formally collect pupils after lunch and there is the opportunity to exchange a few words with SMSAs. (See, for example, Box 3.2 on p. 34.)

Guidance is also available in publications, for example *A Handbook for Lunchtime Supervisors and their Managers* (Rose, 2006) concerns health and safety, child protection, games and activities, preventing bullying and other matters.

University courses for teachers and others

Several universities offer continuing professional development courses, some of which are worthy of consideration by experienced staff working in special schools, including teachers, teaching assistants, residential social workers, nurses, psychologists and others. Courses include ones leading to a postgraduate diploma, postgraduate certificate, and a master's degree or to mandatory qualifications. They may be full-time or part-time and some are delivered by distance education (typically involving study booklets, web-based materials, face-to-face or web-based tutorials, study days, residential weekends and visits).

As courses offered alter from time to time and fees and arrangements may change, a special school may wish to use the university website to request the most recent information. It may also wish to consider how effectively lecturers running the courses have articulated, for example in what they have published, a sufficient understanding of the complex work of special schools. The following focuses mainly on examples of courses that may be suitable for experienced teachers working in special schools. The examples are not intended to be exhaustive and special schools may also wish to contact their most local university to ascertain the courses that are offered there that may also be worth considering.

Box 3.2 ST ANTHONY'S SCHOOL, WEST SUSSEX

St Anthony's School, (www.st-anthony.w-sussex.sch.uk) Chichester, West Sussex is a co-educational local authority community day school for 200 pupils aged 4 to 16 years having autistic spectrum disorder, moderate learning difficulties and speech and language difficulties.

The school's motto 'learning together' is intended to indicate that staff, parents and pupils continually learn so that the school can best educate and care for pupils. In 2001, the school created three tiers of associate staff, i.e. staff not having qualified teacher status: teaching assistants, specialist support assistants (SSAs) and associate teachers.

Teaching assistants support teaching staff with tasks such as the primary care of pupils, playground duties, preparing resources, filing, telephone calls and displays. SSAs work to support the education of a small key worker group (which supports personalised learning) delivering and supervising work set by a qualified teacher. Associate teachers are paid a newly qualified teacher salary; have planning, preparation and assessment time; laptops; and all the status of a teacher. They lead a whole school area such as communication, behaviour, autism, specific literacy difficulty intervention, work-related learning or paramedical care; have additional experience and qualifications in their area; and lead a team of teaching assistants and SSAs. Some move on to join the graduate teaching programme and achieve qualified teacher status but most prefer to stay with their specialism and develop it further. Qualified teachers are responsible for the learning and quality of work but do not deliver all of it enabling them to develop their subject specialisms and allowing the team of staff to differentiate and personalise the education provided.

As a result of these developments, the school has a diverse staff team and a higher pupil : adult ratio than previously. The school has developed existing staff, recruited new ones and retained many who see career progression routes that were not available before, recognising they will have the continuing professional development they require to develop their knowledge and skills.

Postgraduate and/or masters courses are offered by the University of Birmingham (www.education.bham.ac.uk) in 'autism (children)'; 'dyslexia studies'; 'hearing impairment' (which can lead to General Teaching Council recognition as a qualified teacher of the deaf); 'learning difficulties/disabilities (severe, profound and complex)'; 'multisensory impairment' (which, with some additional activities, meets requirements for the DfES mandatory qualification for teachers of children with multi-sensory impairment); 'social, emotional and behavioural difficulties' (using the Training and Development Agency's competencies for core and expert standards for working with pupils with BESD); 'speech and language difficulties'; 'visual impairment: mandatory qualification for teachers of children with a visual impairment'; and 'early years: sensory and multiple needs'.

Edge Hill College of Higher Education (www.edgehill.ac.uk/cpd) provides continuing professional development opportunities for schools and experienced teachers and other professionals. It works in partnership with local authorities (e.g. Lancashire, Cheshire, Wirral) enabling teachers to gain accreditation towards a postgraduate award through daytime, twilight and online learning delivered at a range of local venues. Tutors work with head teachers, advanced skills teachers and others to provide the courses. The postgraduate programme offers part-time modular courses for teachers and others in 'autistic spectrum disorder', 'social, emotional and behavioural difficulties' or 'inclusive education and SEN' leading to a postgraduate certificate, a postgraduate diploma or an MA.

Oxford Brookes University (www.brookes.ac.uk/education) Westminster Institute of Education courses include a Postgraduate Certificate in Advanced Educational Practice in a range of SEN areas including: 'literacy difficulties' and in 'working with children with social, emotional and behavioural difficulties' intended for experienced teachers working with children and young people with SEN. These courses take one year to 19 months involving up to 90 hours, which may include twilight, day, half day and intensive sessions with online resource-based learning. Working with Mary Hare Grammar School for the Deaf, Oxford Brookes offers a Postgraduate Diploma in Educational Studies (Hearing Impairment).

London University Institute of Education (www.ioe.ac.uk) courses include a BEd (Honours) Degree suitable for both teachers and teaching assistants and which includes elements of 'concepts and contexts of SEN'; 'learning, social, emotional and behavioural difficulties'; and 'psychology for education'. There is a graduate diploma/certificate in 'Special and Inclusive Education' for teachers and others wanting to develop skills and expertise in working with children or adults with SEN. A graduate Diploma in 'Special and Inclusive Education (Disabilities of Sight)' meeting the Training and Development Agency National Specialist Standards in Visual Impairment and leading to the DfES mandatory qualification (visual impairment). There is an MA/MSc in 'Special Education (Inclusion and Disability Studies)'. An MA/MSc in 'Special Education (Psychological Perspectives)', which includes an optional module in 'leadership and management in special education'. Also the Special Educational Needs Joint Initiative for Training (SENJIT) involves a partnership between the Institute of Education and LAs to provide short courses, support groups, local training and consultancy for teachers and others working in special education and inclusion.

Sheffield Hallam University (www.shu.ac.uk) is the base for an Autism Centre (www.shu.ac.uk/education/theautismcentre) aiming to facilitate the development of services for people with autistic spectrum disorder and their carers through education and research. Modular courses lead to a postgraduate diploma or to an MA in 'Education of Children and Young People with Autism'. Various modules contribute to meeting the relevant National Special Educational Needs Specialist Standards. A part-time postgraduate certificate run in collaboration with the National Autistic Society is offered in Asperger's syndrome and comprises study modules and a work-based study unit.

Manchester University (www.manchester.ac.uk) provides a part-time 'distributed learning' Diploma/MSc course in 'profound learning disability and multi-sensory impairment'. It offers a full-time course leading to qualification as teacher of the deaf: the Advanced Studies in the Education of Hearing Impaired Children and part-time courses leading to the University Diploma in Advanced Studies in the Education of Hearing Impaired Children (also available as a distance-learning course).

Among its courses, the University of Hertfordshire (www.herts.ac.uk) offers a postgraduate Diploma/MA (Ed.) in the Education of the Hearing Impaired/Deaf full- or part-time. Completion of the postgraduate diploma leads to the mandatory qualification for teachers of the deaf.

Within its MA/diploma courses the University of Northampton (www.northampton.ac.uk) includes modules in autistic spectrum disorder; severe learning difficulty/profound and multiple learning difficulty; speech and language difficulties; and behavioural, emotional and social difficulties. The courses are taught both in Northampton and for LAs in other locations including Derbyshire, Lincolnshire, Leicestershire, Milton Keynes, Bedfordshire and Buckinghamshire.

The University of Leeds (www.leeds.ac.uk) runs a two-year distance-learning course leading to an MA/postgraduate Diploma in Deaf Education (teacher of the deaf). A postgraduate Certificate on 'Provision for Children with Developmental Disorders' concerns developmental coordination disorder, dyslexia, autistic spectrum disorder and attention deficit/hyperactivity disorder.

Cambridge University Faculty of Education (www.educ.cam.ac.uk) courses include an introduction to counselling 60-hour course whose target audience includes special school teachers. The faculty also develops and runs courses in partnership with schools, which may be held elsewhere in the region. The Faculty of Education also has an inclusive and special education research group and the website may be consulted (under the research groups section) to see if any of the work might be useful to special schools.

The University of Worcester (www.worcester.ac.uk) offers a modular MA in Special and Inclusive Education. The modules tend to be thematic and generic rather than specialist, although the development of an autism-specific module was under consideration for 2007. Barrs Court is negotiating with it for the school to provide accredited satellite training.

Kingston University (www.kingston.ac.uk), in partnership with Whitefield Schools and Centre, London, has a part-time postgraduate diploma in multi-sensory impairment involving weekly sessions at Whitefield (www.whitefield.org.uk/training).

Canterbury Christ Church University (www.canterbury.ac.uk) has courses on specific learning difficulties; social, emotional and behavioural difficulties; and on communication difficulties.

The Open University (www.open.ac.uk) courses include ones that can be counted towards an MA in Education (Special Needs/Inclusive Education) such as 'Difficulties in literacy development' and 'Managing behaviour in schools', intended for qualified teachers and other professionals in mainstream or special schools.

Local authority courses

Some local authorities offer courses including accredited courses that may be suitable for special school staff. These may be planned and delivered in cooperation with special schools themselves or with universities and others. Maintained special schools will know the courses offered by their own LA but it may also be worthwhile considering courses run by neighbouring LAs.

Independent and non-maintained special schools may also wish to contact the LA in which their school is situated and LAs in the near neighbourhood to see what is offered, taking particular care that courses are not solely designed for local maintained special schools. Involvement in such training can also improve links between the LA and the non-maintained or independent special school.

Private companies and training for special school staff

Among private companies in England offering training that includes courses and conferences some of which may be suitable for special school staff are:

AWLED Consultancy Ltd., PO Box 33, Newquay, Cornwall TR7 1YP.
    e-mail: enquiries@awled.co.uk; website: www.awled.co.uk.

Inclusive Technology Ltd., Gatehead Business Park, Delph New Road,
    Delph, Oldham OL3 5BX, tel: 01457 819 790;
    website: www.inclusivetechnology.co.uk.

Lighthouse Professional Development, Monkhurst House, Sandy Cross
    Lane, Heathfield, East Sussex TN21 8QR, tel: 0800 587 8880;
    website: www.lighthouse.tv.

Prime Professional Conferences, Prime House, 108 Princess Park Avenue,
    London NW11 0JX tel: 0208 455 980;
    website: www.primeprofessionalconferences.com.

Charitable organisations

Some charitable organisations are involved in training that may be relevant to staff in special schools, as the following examples indicate.

The charity I-CAN (www.ican.org.uk), as well as running its own special schools, organises training relating to speech and language matters that is shared by different professionals. A joint professional framework was developed (I-CAN, 2001) intended to encourage better liaison between teachers and speech and language therapists. It provides a structure to underpin joint training for the two professions in two ways. First, it defines areas of professional competence and knowledge, understanding and skill enabling the two professions to work effectively in an educational setting with the 'speech, language and communication needs' of pupils (ibid.: 5). Also, the framework gives an outline of professional development that can be followed collaboratively by both teachers and speech and language therapists. In the I-CAN website, see under 'contact us' for the e-mail address for training and professional development. The Association of All Speech-impaired Children – AFASIC (www.afasic.org.uk) provides details of courses on its website as they are announced.

The British Institute of Learning Disability (BILD) (www.bild.org.uk), an independent charity, aims to improve the quality of life for people with a learning disability in the United Kingdom, including seeking to advance education and research and to promote ways of working for and with people with a learning disability. It provides learning opportunities and accreditation within the social sector and has provided training and conferences for special school staff, special educational needs coordinators and teachers, therapists and support staff. BILD works in partnership with the National Association of Special Educational Needs, the University of Birmingham Faculty of Education and the University of Worcester giving students on the Foundation Degree in Health and Social Care the opportunity to obtain level 4 national vocational qualifications specific to learning disability. It also provides training, support and advice in the management of behaviour for the education sector. BILD is piloting a self-review process aimed at special schools and mainstream schools looking at outcomes from The Quality Network for children and young people. The Quality Network is an approach aiming to improve the quality of life of people with a learning disability including helping support reviews and developing services for children and young people.

Among other charities offering training, Sense (www.sense.org.uk) Family Education Advisory Service in Sense South East runs courses for teachers of deafblind children. A five-day course that normally runs in spring and autumn is 'A Practical Introduction to Working with Learners who are Deafblind'. Other one-day courses with titles such as 'The Role of Touch in Learning' are offered at other times. While the Dyspraxia Foundation (www.dyspraxia foundation.org.uk) does not run courses, it organises an annual general meeting/parents' conference and every two years a professional conference.

Readers may wish to consult the websites of other charities and organisations to get a picture of what is offered before e-mailing the organisation with specific queries about the suitability of specific courses for experienced and qualified special school staff.

Special schools training

Training schools

Training schools develop and disseminate good practice in initial teacher training (ITT) and the continuing professional development of their staff and undertake research. They work collaboratively with others including LEAs, other schools, higher education institutions and other ITT providers, receiving extra money through the Standards Fund to conduct their training activities. From July 2005, participation in the Training School Programme became dependent on the school being (or becoming) a Specialist School.

A training school might:

- encourage flexible and employment-based routes to teaching;
- demonstrate good practice in modular ITT provision;
- develop the range and quality of mentor training;
- demonstrate good use of Information and Communications Technology (ICT) to support training; and
- share good practice with others.

Only a few mainstream schools are designated as training schools (under 260). In May 2006, only two special schools had taken up training school status: Mary Hare and Beaumont Hill. Mary Hare School for the Deaf, Newbury, Berkshire is a non-maintained co-educational day and boarding school for pupils aged 11 to 19 years who have hearing impairment. Beaumont Hill Special School and Technology College is situated in Darlington, County Durham. Also, training school status (www.standards.dfes.gov.uk/specialist schools/redesignation) was available as a leading option for redesignating specialist schools meeting high performing criteria.

Other approaches to training

A special school may arrange with a university for the school to provide accredited satellite training. For example, Barrs Court School, Hereford (www.barrscourt.hereford.sch.uk) is negotiating with the University of Worcester (www.worcester.ac.uk) for such arrangements.

Also, the school may have links with universities and agree courses linked to its own development related to the school's self-evaluation, as the example of Colnbrook School shows (see Box 3.3).

Box 3.3 COLNBROOK SCHOOL, HERTFORDSHIRE

Colnbrook School, Hertfordshire (www.colnbrook.herts.sch.uk) is a co-educational community special school for up to 90 pupils aged 4 to 11 years. About half the pupils have moderate/complex learning difficulties; a quarter have severe learning difficulties; and about a quarter have autistic spectrum disorder. A base for children with marked autism provides for up to ten pupils. For pupils with significant communication difficulties, the school utilises a 'jigsaw' support base, including a sensory room, offering a practical approach to teaching and learning focusing on communication. Selected groups of up to eight children spend sessions with specialist staff, such as a speech and language therapist, in this room for sessions of an hour, some children attending for a session a day, others once or twice a week.

The school has a well-established training programme with Cambridge University who deliver targeted training over the course of an academic year on a theme selected by the school as a result of its own self-evaluation. The programme involves in-service training days, twilight sessions and action research. These lead to staff acquiring formal qualifications tradable towards advanced diplomas. All staff are invited to attend the training as part of the school's performance management procedures. The training has been developed in conjunction with the Cambridge University Faculty of Education. Themes covered have included, with reference to pupils with SEN: delivering literacy and communication; delivering numeracy; and developing personal and social needs.

Networking with other special schools

Special schools themselves hold a wealth of expertise among their staff and those that support them, so one way of developing staff skills and knowledge is to share expertise. A special school for pupils with moderate learning difficulties who finds it has increasing numbers of pupils with BESD may attend specialist training sessions at another special school that principally educates pupils with BESD.

Similarly, special schools can offer training or offer to share their existing training programme with other special schools who may not be as well-developed in specific areas such as provision for pupils with autism, dyslexia, developmental coordination disorder and other types of SEN. Or the training may focus upon aspects such as counselling or developing partnerships with parents that the host special school does particularly well. Also, groups of special schools in an area sometimes arrange their own training days inviting an outside specialist to conduct training.

Through its own contacts and staff, and that of other special schools, the special school can use for training the expertise of speech and language therapists, medical staff, educational and clinical psychologists, social workers, mental health professionals and others.

Special schools pulling the threads together

An early audit aid intended to inform training and continuing professional development, still consulted by some special schools, is the then Teacher Training Agency's *National Special Educational Needs Specialist Standards* (TTA, 1999). In using a range of training to enhance provision and raise standards of pupils' achievement and enhance their development, special schools adopt several strategies. They may coordinate training through the school's self-evaluation and link the provision of training and its outcomes with their performance management procedures. The school will ultimately seek to link the outcomes of training to improvements in education, care and therapy although it may not always be possible to unpick the direct contribution or training from other developments in the school.

Thinking points

Readers may wish to consider:

* the overall strategy of the special school for staff development and accreditation, and its contribution to staff recruitment and retention;
* how effectively school self-evaluation is linked to training requirements and raising pupils' standards.

Key resources

Training and Development Agency for Schools (2006d) *Guidance on the Standards for the Award of HLTA Status*, London, TDA.
    This document may be most helpfully used if read along with other related documents and information from the TDA website.

Rose, S. (2006) *A Handbook for Lunchtime Supervisors and their Managers*, London, David Fulton Publishers.
    This covers health and safety, child protection, games and activities, preventing bullying and other issues.

The Internet address of the universities, companies, charities and other bodies mentioned in this chapter provide further avenues that the special school may wish to explore.

Chicks

Chapter 4

Distinctive provision

Introductlon

This chapter examines aspects of the curriculum that are adapted in special schools giving flexibility in what is taught: curriculum content; the time allocated to subjects and areas of the curriculum; modifying the depth and interrelationships between programmes of study; and developing other features. I briefly look at the use of thinking skills in the curriculum of the special school.

The chapter then considers special schools and pedagogy identified as being effective with groups of pupils with different types of SEN: behavioural, emotional and social difficulties; profound, severe and moderate learning difficulties; specific learning difficulties; communication and interaction difficulties; and sensory impairment and physical disability.

Curriculum flexibility

In considering that aspect of the special school curriculum concerning 'what' is taught, it is possible to examine ways in which the school can ensure its curriculum encourages the greatest progress and well-being among its pupils. Although the curriculum uses as its basis the National Curriculum it is recognised that its interpretation and development can be quite flexible. The curriculum can be reshaped in different ways. Its content can be altered; the time spent on different subjects and areas of the curriculum can be changed; the depth and interrelationships between aspects of schemes of work or programmes of study can be modified; and other features can be developed. Each of these four ways is examined below.

Curriculum content

National strategies have their particular application and lines of development in special schools including the National Literacy Strategy, the National Numeracy Strategy, the Key Stage 3 Strategy and flexibility at Key Stage 4. Indeed if one wanted to highlight a potential strength of special school provision, one could cite the flexibility in the curriculum it can offer. This can be much greater than that in a mainstream school where there is a tension between special educational curricular justifications and other requirements for pupils not having SEN.

But in a special school for pupils with PMLD, for example, the curriculum can be designed predominantly at a level below level 1 of the National Curriculum in terms of content with variety and stimulation built in through aspects of methodology. St Margaret's School, The Children's Trust, Surrey (www.thechildrenstrust.org.uk) has developed a curriculum framework with particular emphasis on assessment and Barrs Court School, Hereford (www. barrscourt.hereford.sch.uk) has also devised a curriculum with particular strengths in innovative and stimulating content.

The time allocated to subjects and areas of the curriculum

In a special school, more time than is usual can be given to certain subjects and areas of the curriculum in response to types of SEN. This assumes that the same time is spent in a typical school day, so the emphasis of one or more subjects implies that proportionately less time is spent on other areas, a decision the school will have to balance judiciously.

For pupils with BESD this might include more timetabled time spent on personal, social, health and citizenship education or on aspects of the curriculum encouraging communication and the expression of feelings.

With regard to communication difficulties, extra time may be justified on English and communication more generally; and on drama, music and other subjects encouraging communication of various kinds. In the case of autism, again communication will be a priority.

Provision for pupils with sensory impairment has implications for the time devoted to particular subjects. Visual impairment will suggest extra time being allowed for mobility training within personal, social, health and citizenship education. Some physical disabilities may indicate extra time spent on physical education, perhaps involving movement development through conductive education.

For pupils with PMLD, extra time will be spent on core areas such as communication, cognition and personal and social development. For pupils with specific learning difficulties time allocations can differ. For example, for pupils with dyslexia, extra time may be allocated to areas of the curriculum likely to help compensate for a supposed phonological deficit such as speech and language skills in English and other subjects.

Modifying the depth and interrelationships between programmes of study

As well as extra time being allocated, interrelationships between different subjects can be particularly carefully planned.

For pupils with BESD, the programmes of study for say English; drama; and personal, social, health and citizenship education can be scrutinised and aspects relating to the articulating of feelings highlighted. This is so that an aspect of what in current terminology is referred to as 'emotional literacy' is built in to studies, that of developing a vocabulary for feelings and learning to use it. Extra time is not allocated, but teachers ensure that this thread of the curriculum is covered and is given emphasis as it arises so that the pupils are encouraged to make connections between the skills of expressing feelings through English, drama and other subjects.

With regard to communication difficulties, a similar scrutiny of schemes of work can help ensure that, for example, difficulties with grammar are tackled through the grammatical aspects of subjects being lifted to the surface (passive voice in science, particular grammatical strings used routinely in history or geography). With regard to autistic spectrum disorder, tracking of threads of subjects can highlight semantic-pragmatic elements.

Where a pupil is deafblind, the curriculum emphasises elements concerning communication (for example symbolic and non-symbolic communication, and the use of communication in activities and group work); mobility; and finding out information and encouraging meaningful experiences.

For pupils with moderate learning difficulties, extra time will be spent on the areas of literacy, numeracy and perhaps information and communications technology. For a pupil with dyscalculia, clearly elements of subjects that reinforce mathematical understanding will be mapped out. For example science, physical education, geography, design and technology are all important contributors to mathematical knowledge and understanding.

Developing other features

Extra time and better interrelationships of schemes of work can be further supplemented by allocating time to other features of the curriculum that may not always be expressed in relation to the National Curriculum.

For pupils with BESD, other provision might include anger management sessions, psychotherapy, art therapy and other elements aimed at encouraging the expression and understanding of feelings and the management of behaviour.

With regard to communication difficulties, extra time can be allocated to specific sessions with a speech and language therapist, for example working on articulation. For pupils with autistic spectrum disorder, there may be sessions of behaviour management aimed at helping the pupil gain access to the provision such as aspects of the Lovaas programme.

For a pupil with motor difficulties there may be extra sessions devoted to physiotherapy or occupational therapy, developing skills in different contexts.

In practice, aspects of these are integrated into the curriculum as it is experienced in the classroom, perhaps with a teacher and therapy specialist working together on planning and delivery. A physiotherapist and a teacher will plan the content of sessions aimed at developing better movement skills and work together in the classroom with the pupils. A speech and language therapist and a teacher may similarly work on articulation skills development programmes to be delivered while working together, perhaps taught by the teacher and specially trained learning support assistant under the speech and language therapist's guidance.

Thinking skills

A thinking skills approach to teaching emphasises the processes of thinking and learning such as information processing, enquiry, making distinctions and connections, forming hypotheses, and evaluation and their generalisation. To the extent that it is considered a facilitator of pupil autonomy, thinking skills are sometimes considered as an aspect of pupil participation (see also Chapter 9 'Dynamic pupil participation').

In pioneering work, Feuerstein developed a set of activities ('instruments') intended to enable an adult to help children's learning processes (Feuerstein, 1979). Particular tasks were aimed at tackling underlying difficulties in functioning. The programme, Instrumental Enrichment (IE), is generally used with groups where there is opportunity to use discussion and experience evidence of the way others are thinking. The more basic concepts and skills involved are later reintroduced in a spiral curriculum at a higher conceptual level. The teacher acts as a mediator to help the pupil connect the IE materials and other areas of learning (Feuerstein *et al.*, 1980; Sharon and Coulter, 1994; Romney and Samuels, 2001).

Mathew Lipman, founder of the Institute for the Advancement of Philosophy for Children (IAPC) at Montclair State College, New Jersey developed materials for school children aged six years to secondary school age and the approach known as philosophy for children (P4C). The IAPC has produced novels, encouraging pupils to raise questions and forming the grounding for guided discussion. Children in the novels are also involved in discussions and exploratory thinking (Lipman *et al.*, 1980).

In the United Kingdom, the *Somerset Thinking Skills Course* (Blagg *et al.*, 1988) elaborated and updated the IE approach. Another programme, *Top Ten Thinking Tactics*, is cross-related to the National Curriculum and includes skills such as 'systematic search' and 'pinpointing the problem' (Lake and Needham, 1990). Research into thinking skills in relation to science and mathematics and other subjects has been carried out (Adey and Shayer, 2002); resources have been developed to encourage philosophical enquiry (Fisher, 1998); and a Society for the Advancement of Philosophical Enquiry and Reflection in Education was founded (Murris and Haynes, 2000). Aspects of thinking skills are part of the National Curriculum.

A summary of some of the research and issues is provided in a Department for Education and Skills report (McGuinness, 1999) (www.dfes.gov.uk/research/data/uploadfiles/RB115.doc) which in reviewing classroom evaluation studies suggests unsurprisingly that not all approaches are equally effective and that: 'the more successful approaches tend to have a strong theoretical underpinning, well designed and contextualised materials, explicit pedagogy and good teaching support' (ibid.: 1).

Special schools may wish to examine the extent to which a particular approach assumes that knowledge and understanding are socially constructed, regarding thinking skills as particularly important so pupils come to recognise the supposed subjective and socially determined nature of educational content. This might lead special schools to consider whether such a view lends itself better to some aspects of its curriculum than others.

The special school may also wish to review the work that has been taking place for many years in relation to aspects of thinking skills, for example that on metacognition with pupils having severe or profound learning difficulties articulated in curriculum documents at Rectory Paddock School, Bromley (www.rectorypaddock.bromley.sch.uk) in the 1980s.

It may be necessary to be alert to jargon around critical thinking disguising the glaring obviousness of what is being done. For example, the DfES standards site (www.standards.dfes.gov.uk) in 2006 gave a glossary of terms including 'mediation' which is defined as: 'a teaching strategy where the teacher intervenes and supports the development of pupils' understanding by modelling or by direct instruction to help them achieve something they could not do alone.' It is very difficult to distinguish between this technical intervention and a teacher simply showing a pupil what to do, although to be fair a fuller definition might have done more justice to the underpinnings of these approaches. But some definitions in the glossary appear to have been provided for teachers who have been living on Mars for 20 years and include: 'problem solving', 'reasoning' and 'dialogue' ('shared enquiry between two or more people').

Another consideration is how thinking skills might be taught: as discrete general sessions, applied to particular subjects or areas of the curriculum (e.g. thinking skills in science); or an across-the-curriculum approach (e.g. McGuinness, 1999: 2). These are similar to the decisions relating to teaching and learning information and communication technology.

Special schools and distinctive provision

Many of the points discussed above are evident where special schools develop a distinctive provision for pupils with particular types of SEN.

Behavioural, emotional and social difficulties

In relation to BESD, interventions may be broadly described in systemic, cognitive, behavioural and psychodynamic terms (Farrell, 2006a).

Systemic perspectives lead to examining the child's environment and other factors before assuming 'within child' factors are influential and have included approaches such as family therapy, intensive home–school liaison, circle of friends and circle time (ibid.: ch. 2). Cognitive views emphasise the role of a child's perceptions and thinking process and are associated with aspects of emotional literacy, anxiety management and self talk (ibid.: ch. 3). Behavioural approaches, focusing on the externals of behaviour, may involve schedules of reinforcement of behaviour and techniques such as modelling and desensitisation and vehicles such as contracts and social skills training (ibid.: ch. 4). Psychodynamic views associated with unconscious conflicts and the powerful impact of childhood experiences may be part of therapies (play, art, music, drama, movement), psychodynamic counselling and nurture groups (ibid.: ch. 5). Regarding specific aspects of BESD, distinctive pedagogies are also emerging as, for example, with attention deficit hyperactivity disorder where aspects include providing a structured environment with stimulating learning tasks and minimum disruptions, allowing optimum breaks in classroom work and perhaps using biofeedback devices to help the pupil recognise feelings at an early stage and manage them better (ibid.: ch. 6).

Special schools are often eclectic in drawing on these approaches although some are well known for particular expertise in one or two approaches. Chelfham Mill School, Devon (www.chelfhammillschool.co.uk) was an early exponent of behavioural approaches, although later including cognitive and psychodynamic elements into its provision (Farrell, 2006f: 65). The Mulberry Bush School (www.mulberrybush.oxon.sch.uk), Oxfordshire developed its psychodynamic orientation from the work of its founder Barbara Dockar Drysdale (Farrell, 2006f: 66).

Profound, severe and moderate learning difficulties

For pupils with profound, severe or moderate learning difficulties, there are both differences in pedagogy and areas of overlap; one feature distinguishing provision being curriculum and assessment level. For pupils with MLD, curriculum and assessment reflects the greater difficulty the pupils have than peers in acquiring basic literacy and numeracy skills and understanding concepts. For pupils with SLD, the curriculum and assessment level is indicated by the pupils' levels of attainment being within performance indicator scales P4 to P8. For pupils with PMLD, attainments are likely to be within P scale range 1 to 4 throughout their school careers.

For pupils with MLD, the curriculum tends to be subject-based and practically orientated with provision for literacy such as Reading Intervention. Concrete and visual apparatus, first-hand experience and relevance to everyday life are emphasised. Opportunities for exploratory learning and investigation are provided with structure as necessary and the pace of lessons ensures that learning is secure. Where pupils with MLD experience additional difficulties

---

Box 4.1 FITZWARYN SCHOOL, OXFORDSHIRE

Fitzwaryn School, Wantage, Oxfordshire is a community co-educational day school educating 62 pupils aged 2 to 16 years having moderate, severe or profound learning difficulties, about a third of whom have autistic spectrum disorder. The school's awards include the Basic Skills Agency award; an International award and two Department for Education and Skills excellence awards.

The school runs an integrated foundation-stage class within a local primary school and Fitzwaryn also piloted a local early years outreach project. Therefore most pupils coming into Fitzwaryn have already experienced appropriate early intervention. All lower school children spend time in local mainstream schools as appropriate. Wherever possible, pupils undertake work experience and the school is currently developing enterprise education for the senior pupils.

There is a cohesive method of teaching, learning and assessment, which are all interlinked. This enables personalised learning pathways to be devised as a result of assessments made and any data collected is used to improve provision for individuals. Each teacher identifies levels of pupil achievement and sets challenging individual pupil targets, which are regularly reviewed. These targets then form the basis of planning for groups and curriculum areas within the National Curriculum framework. The use of information and communication technology and developing methods of using 'Assessment for Learning' are emphasised across the curriculum.

Its focus is on developing a whole school communication environment involving 'communication' as an element of individual education plans as appropriate. Fitzwaryn is looking at ways of improving pupil participation and in 2006 introduced a visual annual review format to enable pupils to play an active role in reviews.

in the areas of behaviour and communication, the curriculum and provision take account of these (Farrell, 2006b: ch. 2). Among many examples of schools having aspects of these approaches are Alfriston School, Buckinghamshire and Sutton School, Dudley (Farrell, 2006f: 67–8). (See also, for example, Box 4.1.)

Turning to SLD, the curriculum and teaching and learning approaches include adapting the National Curriculum and strategies such as the National Literacy Strategy; maximising cross-curricular links; and setting intermediate targets. Assessment may involve small-steps scales and records such as P scales, B Squared or PIVATS and Records of Achievement. Teaching and learning are likely to include multi-sensory methods, interactive approaches, visual methods, augmentative and alternative communication, encouraging communication through music, using ICT to enhance curriculum access and having regular routines (Farrell, 2006b: chs 3 and 4). (See, for example, Box 4.2.)

With regard to PMLD, the curriculum will tend to balance the school's response to the subject-based National Curriculum and the perceived developmental and learning requirements of the pupils. Assessment takes into account small steps of vertical progress, but also horizontal progress, for example in the experience of a breadth of activities. Schools also use multi-sensory approaches; link resources to routines; emphasise and encourage communication; and encourage pupils to control their surroundings (Farrell, 2006b: ch. 5). Many schools educate pupils with PMLD and SLD (and sometimes pupils with MLD) in the same school and draw on the approaches described, examples being St Luke's School, Scunthorpe (Farrell, 2006f: 69–70) and William Harvey School, North London (Farrell, 2006f: 70–1) (www.portables.ngfl.gov.uk/dwgodfrey/). (See also, for example, Box 4.3.)

Specific learning difficulties

There is debate about what is to be included in the range of specific learning difficulties. Here I touch on dyslexia, dyspraxia/developmental coordination disorder, and dyscalculia.

With reference to dyslexia, approaches include those for supposed underlying difficulties such as phonological deficit (raising the pupil's phonological awareness in lessons, providing speech and language therapy). Other interventions focus directly on the difficulties with reading, writing and spelling where, for instance, reading approaches may combine phonological training with reading (Farrell, 2006c: chs 2 and 3). Mark College, Somerset (www.markcollege.somerset.sch.uk) is an example of a school educating pupils with dyslexia (Farrell, 2006f: 72).

Turning to dyspraxia, education includes particular work and interventions for handwriting; personal, social, health and citizenship education; and physical education. For example in handwriting strategies, seek to ensure a correct writing posture, a good pencil grip and improved hand–eye coordination (Farrell, 2006c: ch. 4).

Box 4.2 HERITAGE HOUSE SCHOOL, CHESHAM, BUCKINGHAMSHIRE

Heritage House School (www.heritagehouse.bucks.sch.uk), Chesham, Buckinghamshire is a community special school for pupils aged 2 to 19 years with complex learning difficulties or severe learning difficulties. It joined a consortium of six local schools to form a sports college allowing the school to develop a specialism in dance, drama and creative arts and to have opportunities for individual pupils to receive specialist coaching. Health Trust staff working in the school include a physiotherapist and speech and language therapists. The school's 'skills for life' curriculum includes core areas monitored using the school's own assessment materials, which assess progress against performance descriptor scales.

The areas are: effective communication (which includes teachers working with the speech and language therapist, and the use of Picture Exchange Communication Systems (PECs) to support communication); practical skills of independence, which include encouraging pupils to inform others when they can do things and the school's own Safety in the Community test; personal and social development; problem solving, including making choices; physical fitness, including physiotherapy and for a few pupils a MOVE curriculum; and sports and arts including Tai Chi, drumming and tag rugby.

The school is organised into an early learning department (2 to 7 years) whose curriculum has an additional emphasis on sensory learning; a main school department (7 to 14) and an extended education department (14 to 19). There is a flexible grouping of pupils according to their stage of learning in a subject or for particular sessions such as MOVE (Mobility Opportunities Via Education®).

The four classes in the TEACCH department educate pupils aged 5 to 19 years who have autistic spectrum disorder, integrating their pupils in varying degrees with the rest of the school. All teachers and some teaching assistants have been trained in TEACCH and the parents' support group is examining ways of adapting the approach to home use.

As well as the classes in the TEACCH department following the TEACCH approach, all the other classes use the framework with one or more pupils to mediate their interaction with their surroundings and make it more comprehensible.

Within the TEACCH department, the major priorities include centring on the individual and their understanding of and interaction with their environment and a broadly based intervention strategy that builds on the pupil's existing skills and interests. Emphasis is placed on individualised assessment to understand the pupil better and to build programmes around their functioning.

Box 4.3 BIDWELL BROOK SCHOOL, DEVON

Bidwell Brook School, Devon (www.bidwellbrook.devon.sch.uk) is a community co-educational school educating up to 88 pupils aged 3 to 19 years with severe or profound and multiple learning difficulties. The school is part of a federation with a local primary school and a community college. Particular curriculum strengths are information and communication technology, Personal, Social, Health and Citizenship Education (PSHCE), art and design and music.

Throughout the school, a sensory and therapeutic curriculum encompasses speech and language therapy, occupational therapy, psychotherapy, hydrotherapy, aromatherapy, and the use of multi-sensory environments, movement, and rebound therapy. These approaches, individualised for particular pupils, lead to programmes for communication, body awareness, mobility, and control over the environment. For pupils who have not developed the use of language and are difficult to reach, intensive interaction is used. Manual signing, the picture exchange communication system, and rebus symbols are used to encourage communication.

At the foundation stage (3 to 4 years) the school has its own curriculum based on early learning goals, and pupils are assessed using performance indicators (P scales), EQUALS and B Squared assessments.

In Key Stage 1, (5 to 7 years) the curriculum is based on topic areas such as 'ourselves and senses' and 'journeys, transport and our world'. At Key Stage 2, (7 to 11) the curriculum is more subject based.

In the secondary department, the emphasis is on literacy, numeracy and social skills. Independent living skills become an increasingly central feature as pupils grow older. Pupils are assessed, using as appropriate P scales and OCR Accreditation for Life and Living and the National Skills Profile.

In educating pupils with dyscalculia, interventions include those drawing on approaches to education for dyslexia and dyspraxia to the degree that it is judged that the mathematics difficulties arise from underlying difficulties common with them. Other interventions more specific to dyscalculia include: teaching prerequisite skills in classification, length, area and volume (Farrell, 2006c: ch. 5).

Communication and interaction difficulties

The education of pupils with communication difficulties can be viewed in relation to difficulties with speech, grammar, meaning, the use of language and language comprehension in which the role of a speech and language therapist is important.

Difficulties with speech may concern the speech elements of phonology, phonetics and prosody and interventions may comprise the teacher raising phonological awareness in lessons, for instance asking how different sounds blend together and break up.

Problems with grammar (morphology and syntax) are helped by such means as the teacher ensuring she communicated directly and effectively and through supporting the development of grammatical utterances through reading and writing activities.

Difficulties with meaning (semantics) may involve problems with labelling, packaging and network building (working out how one word relates to another), understanding idioms, understanding grammar and understanding the meaning of relations. Effective education includes providing structured experiences to help the pupil build an understanding of different labelling words, and analysing and correcting through practical experience when a learner is under-extending or over-extending a label.

Problems with language use (pragmatics) relates to grammatical sense in the use of language and social and linguistic sense. The teacher might give support by helping the child develop conversational skills, and assisting with difficulties in the social and linguistic sense in communication by, for example, explaining and modelling conventions.

Language comprehension difficulties involve the roles of grammar and attention in relation to comprehension. Provision includes modelling listening behaviour and showing the pupil how to assertively indicate lack of understanding in lessons (Farrell, 2006d: chs 2 to 6).

Dawn House School, Nottinghamshire (www.ican.org.uk) (Farrell, 2006f: 76) uses a language-based curriculum and other features while Woodsetton School, Dudley (www.woodsetton.dudley.gov.uk) uses the Derbyshire Language Scheme. Both schools place great importance on close working between the speech and language therapist and other staff (Farrell, 2006f: 76–7).

Provision for pupils with autistic spectrum disorder responds to the triad of impairments (social isolation, communication difficulties, insistence of sameness) and includes approaches drawing on interventions such as TEACCH; the Lovaas programme; and intensive interaction. Musical interaction therapy aims to develop the pupil's ability to enjoy the company of others and his understanding of how to interact and communicate (Farrell, 2006d: ch. 7). Freemantles School, Surrey (Farrell, 2006f: 78) and Peterhouse School, Southport (www.autisminitiatives.org) (Farrell, 2006f: 78–9) are among schools that illustrate some of these approaches.

Sensory impairment and physical disability

Educating learners with hearing impairment includes paying particular attention to communication and literacy. A particular school may have a preference for oral/aural; total communication or sign bilingual approaches

(Farrell, 2006e: ch. 3). An example of a school specialising in educating pupils with hearing impairments is The Royal School for the Deaf and Communication Disorders, Stockport (www.rdsmanchester.org) (Farrell, 2006f: 80).

Provision for pupils with visual impairment includes suitable lighting and low-vision devices; Braille or Moon (a tactile medium based on a raised line adaptation of the Roman print alphabet); enabling pupils to gain efficient access to information; and training in orientation and mobility (Farrell, 2006e: ch. 2).

Turning to learners who are deafblind, again special attention is given to communication, for example using hand-over-hand work; resonance work (involving an adult reflecting back to the child movements or vocalisations); and co-creative communication (emphasising the relationship between the child and a communication partner) (Farrell, 2006e: ch. 4).

One school that educates pupils who are blind or deafblind is The Royal School for the Blind, Liverpool (www.rsblind.org.uk) (Farrell, 2006f: 81).

Regarding conditions associated with physical and motor disability, medical conditions have to be provided for. Education interventions include: adaptations to the environment; curricular emphases such as personal, social, health and citizenship education; flexible routines; and programmes to develop and consolidate motor skills including physiotherapy and motor training (Farrell, 2006e: ch. 5). Schools educating learners with physical and motor disabilities include Treloar School, Hampshire (www.treloar.org.uk) (Farrell, 2006f: 83–4) and Fairfields School, Northampton (http://atschool.eduweb.co.uk/fairfieldsFairfields_School_ie.htm) (Farrell, 2006f: 84–5).

Thinking points

The school may wish to consider:

- refinements in its curriculum content; time allocated to subjects and areas of the curriculum; the depth and interrelationships between programmes of study;
- its effectiveness in development of thinking skills;
- the relationship of its provision to the main SEN of its pupils.

Key texts

Farrell, M. (2006a) *The Effective Teacher's Guide to Behavioural, Emotional and Social Difficulties*, London, Routledge.

Farrell, M. (2006b) *The Effective Teacher's Guide to Moderate, Severe and Profound Learning Difficulties*, London, Routledge.

Farrell, M. (2006c) *The Effective Teacher's Guide to Dyslexia and Other Specific Learning Difficulties*, London, Routledge.

Farrell, M. (2006d) *The Effective Teacher's Guide to Autism and Other Communication Difficulties*, London, Routledge.

Farrell, M. (2006e) *The Effective Teacher's Guide to Sensory Impairment and Physical Disability*, London, Routledge.

These books form a series covering the main types of SEN and the provision associated with them.

Cooking

Chapter 5

Better children's well-being

Introduction

Encouraging a child's well-being and safety, while important in its own right, also relates intimately to academic achievement and personal and social development. Aspects such as child safety and well-being are self-evidently important. A child who feels safe and positive about himself is also more likely to be able to achieve better than otherwise in school and to develop better personally, emotionally and socially.

This is reflected in the English system in the development of the Every Child Matters (ECM) programme which relates to aspects of school self-evaluation such as teaching and learning and curriculum provision.

In this chapter, I look at the Children Act 2004; Every Child Matters and SEN; and ECM and special school self-evaluation and inspection. Relating to this, I look at care, guidance and support from the perspective implicit in Office for Standards in Education (OfSTED) guidance and at some implications for special schools.

The Children Act 2004

A report on the death of a young girl who was abused and killed by her great aunt and the man they lived with led to recognition of the need for better integration and accountability across children's services. Accordingly, a government consultation Green Paper *Every Child Matters* was published in 2003 followed by the document *Every Child Matters: The Next Steps* and the Children Act 2004. The Act was intended to form the legislative basis for developing more accessible and effective services around the needs of children, young people and their families. The main provisions of the Act were:

- a Children's Commissioner to represent the views and interests of children and young people;
- a duty on local authorities to arrange to promote cooperation between agencies and other bodies to improve children's well-being and a duty on key partners to take part in cooperation arrangements;

- a duty on key agencies to safeguard and promote the welfare of children;
- a duty on local authorities to set up Local Safeguarding Children Boards and on key partners to take part;
- provision for databases on information on children and young people to aid information sharing;
- a requirement on each local authority to produce a single Children and Young People's Plan;
- a requirement for each local authority to appoint a Director of Children's Services and designate a lead member;
- the creation of an integrated inspection framework and joint area reviews to assess local areas, progress in improving outcomes; and
- provisions concerning foster care, private fostering and the education of children in care.

Every Child Matters: Change for Children and SEN

Every Child Matters: Change for Children (www.everychildmatters.gov.uk/ information/), the programme concerning the well-being of children and young people from birth to 19 years old, requires that organisations providing services to children, for example hospitals, schools, the police and voluntary groups, work together in more integrated and effective ways. This includes sharing information and working together to protect children and young people from harm and to help them achieve what they want in life. It is intended that children and young people will have more say about issues affecting them. The programme seeks to place better outcomes for children at the centre of policies and approaches involving children's services.

In 2005, a Children's Commissioner for England was appointed. One of their roles was to gather and put forward the views of the most vulnerable children and young people in society and promote their involvement in the work of organisations whose decisions and actions affect them.

From April 2006, directors of children's services and the local authorities developed trust arrangements and statutory Children and Young People's Plans and worked with partners including schools to tackle priorities. All schools are expected to work towards Every Child Matters outcomes through:

- common processes, including the Common Assessment Framework and the new local authority children's database;
- partnership working with a wide cross-section of organisations and people, e.g. the children's trust, parents and the wider community, voluntary groups and the private sector; and
- the new relationship with schools, which addresses ECM outcomes through, for example, personalisation and the new school profile (www. everychildmatters.gov.uk/ete/). (See, for example, Box 5.1.)

Box 5.1 ASPLEY WOOD SCHOOL, NOTTINGHAM

Every Child Matters outcomes

Aspley Wood School, Nottingham (www.aspleywood.nottingham.sch.uk) is a co-educational community special school for 40 pupils with physical disabilities and complex learning difficulties. It has a British Council International School Award; a Schools Curriculum Award (2000 and 2002); a School Achievement Award (2003); a Sport for All Award and has Investors in People recognition. As well as teachers and teaching assistants, the school has its own therapists and nurses and is visited by social workers, a music therapist and a teacher for the deaf.

Regarding ECM outcomes and provision supporting them, pupils are encouraged to adopt healthy lifestyles. They have a daily, individual physical programme with targets set and reviewed by qualified staff. Alternative forms of exercise are offered as appropriate, such as horse riding. All pupils have weekly hydrotherapy/swimming sessions, working through a graded system of small steps for progress in swimming. After-school clubs include team sports. Healthy eating is part of the curriculum and the daily meal menu includes a choice of hot meal or salad; pudding or fruit.

Concerning safe practices, pupils have been involved in an audit of bullying although incidents are extremely rare. The School Council contributed to the policy. All aspects of keeping oneself safe are taught through PSHCE and science. Pupils are consulted about moving and handling (for example feeling safe in a hoist). Staff have training in moving and handling and the correct use of wheelchair clamps and operation of the tail lift on the school buses. Through verbal and non-verbal means, pupils are encouraged throughout their time at school to express preferences and make choices whenever possible. The school has a Pupil Welfare policy specifying that pupils should give informed consent, whenever possible, to therapeutic and intimate care procedures.

In terms of enjoying their education, pupils express positive views in questionnaires and individual interviews. Pupils are caring of each other and verbal pupils will speak up for their non-verbal peers. Effort and achievement are celebrated at the end of each week in department assemblies, age appropriately, for example younger pupils receiving a 'leaf' for their 'achievement tree' while older pupils get a merit card based on key skills. Classes have a 'pause for thought' at some time in the school day with an opportunity to reflect on their own values and feelings.

With reference to learners making a positive contribution to the community, pupils learn about this through the PSHCE curriculum and informally as occasion arises. The leavers' programme covers disability rights, benefits and educational maintenance. Pupils are given opportunities to express their views in the community, for example when older learners took part in a campaign for more accessible toilets in the city centre. Pupils also raise money for charities and other causes decided by the School Council, which meets half termly.

In preparing for their future economic well-being, learners have opportunities to use real money in real contexts as often as possible. In a health and fitness themed week, younger pupils used a tram and a train as part of the termly themed work on transport and bought fruit at a local market. Some IEP targets relate to the understanding of money values, time, timetables and social sight vocabulary. Year 11 pupils have the opportunity of a supported work experience at a city centre theatre. A priority is to ensure pupils have appropriate skills to plan their leisure and have as much control over their lives as possible.

While what was stated earlier applies to all children and young people, for pupils with SEN the ECM programme is meant to encourage a new emphasis on:

- integrating services around children and young people;
- early identification and effective support for children with additional needs; and
- participation by children and young people themselves.

Developments such as pooling budgets and resources and the Common Assessment Framework are meant to contribute.

The programme is intended to reflect the strategies outlined in the document *Removing Barriers to Achievement: The Government's Strategy for SEN* (DfES, 2004c). In developing statutory Children and Young People's Plans, children's trusts are expected to review their policies on SEN and the support available to seek to ensure several aims. These are:

- effective delegation of resources to support early intervention and inclusion;
- reduction of reliance on SEN statements;
- appropriate provision;
- better specialist advice and support to schools and information to parents; and
- a reduction in bureaucracy (www.everychildmatters.gov.uk/ete/sen/).

The National Service Framework

The document *National Service Framework for Children, Young People and Maternity Services: Supporting Local Delivery* (Department for Education and Skills and Department of Health, 2004) includes an outline of the National Service Framework (NSF). The document is intended mainly for health organisations but also their partners including education services and social care. The NSF sets out a ten-year programme, as part of the Every Child Matters strategy, involving setting standards of care of children, young people and the maternity services.

ECM and special school self-evaluation and inspection

The ECM outcomes are set out in the document *Conducting the Inspection: Guidance for Inspectors of Schools* (OfSTED, 2005d: 10, paraphrased) with examples as follows:

1   be healthy (e.g. helping pupils adopt healthy lifestyles, build self-esteem, eat and drink well and lead active lives);
2   stay safe (e.g. keeping learners safe from bullying, harassment and other dangers);
3   enjoy and achieve (e.g. enabling pupils to make good progress in their work and personal development and to enjoy their education);
4   make a positive contribution (e.g. ensuring that learners understand their rights and responsibilities, are listened to, and participate in the life of the community);
5   achieve economic well-being (e.g. helping pupils to gain the skills and knowledge needed for future employment).

Further interpretations of the outcomes are evident in annex A of the inspection judgements form appended to OfSTED school reports. These include, in terms of the extent to which schools enable learners to be healthy, that learners are 'discouraged from smoking and substance abuse' and 'educated about sexual health'. Regarding the extent to which providers ensure that learners stay safe, one aspect is that 'Risk assessment procedures and related staff training are in place'. Turning to the extent to which learners make a positive contribution, one consideration is that learners 'are helped to develop stable, positive relationships'. To the extent to which schools enable learners to achieve economic well-being, an aspect is that 'Careers education and guidance is provided to all learners in Key Stage 3 and 4 and in the sixth form.'

The document *Every Child Matters: Framework for the Inspection of Schools in England from September 2005* (OfSTED, 2005a) draws out connections between the five ECM outcomes and the evaluation requirements of the inspection framework.

In evaluating achievement and standards relating to more academic standards, the outcome focused on is unsurprisingly outcome 3, 'enjoy and achieve through learning'. Where standards relate to personal development and well-being, all five outcomes are referred to in cross-referencing with different aspects as indicated in the following list. The numbers in brackets refer to the five outcomes listed on p. 6:

- the acquisition of workplace skills (4,5);
- the development of skills which contribute to the social and economic well-being of the learners (2,4,5);
- the emotional development of learners (1);
- the behaviour of learners (1,2);
- the attendance of learners (2,3);
- the extent to which learners adopt safe practices and a healthy lifestyle (1,2,5);
- learners' spiritual, moral, social and cultural development (3,4); and
- whether learners make a positive contribution to the community (4).

(OfSTED, 2005a: 19)

In evaluations concerning teaching and learning, again not surprisingly, all are cross-referenced to Every Child Matters outcome 3. One aspect is linked also to outcome 4, 'make a positive contribution to society'. This is the aspect to evaluate: 'how well teaching and/or training and resources promote learning, address the full range of learners' needs and meet course or programme requirements (3,4)' (ibid.: 19).

In evaluating 'how well do programmes and activities meet the needs and interests of learners?' the aspects and Every Child Matters outcomes are as follows:

- the extent to which programmes or activities match learners' aspirations and potential, building on prior attainment and experience (3,5);
- how far programmes or the curriculum meet external requirements and are responsive to local circumstances (4,5);
- the extent to which employers' needs are met (5);
- the extent to which enrichment activities and/or extended services contribute to learners' enjoyment and achievement (3,4,5); and
- the extent to which the provision contributes to the learner's capacity to stay safe and healthy (1,2).

(ibid.: 20)

In judging 'how well are learners guided and supported?' the aspects and links are:

- the care, advice, guidance and other support provided to safeguard welfare, promote personal development and achieve high standards (1,2,3); and
- the quality and accessibility of information and advice and guidance to learners in relation to courses and programmes, and, where applicable, career progression (3,5).

(ibid.: 20)

Turning to 'leadership and management', this is considered to relate to all the Every Child Matters outcomes.

Readers from countries other than England may have similar aims relating to their own pastoral and academic support systems. What is perhaps important is not so much the particular ECM framework for seeking to ensure better outcomes for children in relation to health, safety, enjoyment and achievement, their positive contribution and their economic well-being, but that such a framework and outcomes can be agreed, acted upon and integrated with other aims. (See, for example, Box 5.2.)

Box 5.2 BROOKFIELDS SCHOOL, READING

Brookfields School, Reading is an LEA co-educational school for 190 pupils aged 2 to 19 years and having moderate, severe or profound learning difficulties including some pupils with autism or sensory impairment. The school has an autism and behaviour support service (www.autismatbrookfields.co.uk) and a sensory resource (www.sensoryresource.co.uk) involving partnership with other services including the Royal National Institute for the Blind.

Sport and physical education are important in the school, which has a Sportsmark Award. For example, four lunchtimes per week, pupils in Key Stages 2, 3 and 4 are able to participate in coaching sessions taken by a Football Association coach organised through the soccer in the community project. Key Stage 4 pupils are encouraged to take on positions of leadership in the school through organising charity events, being a member of the schools council or leading the school's three 'houses'.

Using the Every Child Matters outcomes to aid self-evaluation

In many special schools, the provision that will contribute to the outcomes summarised by the ECM programme may already be in place. The outcomes can, however, act as a check and an incentive to developing better provision.

In reflecting on the outcomes and the evidence needed to demonstrate they are being achieved, the school may review its provision and check it is delivering what is expected.

For example, the school can contribute to the outcome 'be healthy' by, among other things, helping pupils eat and drink well. Reviewing provision relating to this is likely to include looking at the food and drink provided by the school at breakfast clubs, lunchtimes and break times (fresh fruit snacks) and at the contents of any vending machines. It may involve auditing what pupils choose at mealtimes and surveying the sorts of healthy food that appeal to them. It could involve considering the related elements of the personal, social, health and citizenship education schemes of work as well as work in biology, physical education and other subject areas.

In its self-evaluation, the special school can use the suggested links outlined earlier to help ensure that outcomes are being encouraged. This can be done by systematically working through the elements of the framework for inspection and finding evidence that ECM outcomes are being supported. For example, in evaluating 'the behaviour of learners' is the school giving sufficient attention to pupils being healthy and staying safe? Another approach is, while planning to work through all aspects of self-evaluation, to begin with areas in which the school considers improvement is required and prioritising these. Where there are no obvious priorities of this kind, the school might begin with the aspects that relate to most outcomes and may therefore be the most complicated to track. For example, 'the care, advice, guidance and other support provided to safeguard welfare, promote personal development and achieve high standards' which relate to outcomes 1, 2 and 3.

Some of the ECM outcomes will involve close working with other agencies. For example, that aspect of 'staying safe' that includes ensuring that procedures for safeguarding learners meet current government requirements is likely to involve multi-agency working with colleagues in the health services, social services and others. The special school should find it helpful to distinguish clearly between the evidence of the outcomes and the provision that is expected to support them.

Care, guidance and support

OfSTED guidance

In England, OfSTED's view of care, guidance and support is conveyed in various sources of guidance on the school inspection process. In using the guidance, *Using the Evaluation Schedule* (OfSTED, 2005b), inspectors evaluate:

• 'the care, advice, guidance and other support provided to safeguard welfare, promote personal development and well-being, and achieve high standards;

- the quality and accessibility of information, advice and guidance to learners in relation to courses and programmes, and, where applicable, to career progression; and
- the extent to which the provision promotes learners' health and ensures their safety'.

(ibid.: 10)

ECM outcomes relate importantly to evaluation of care, guidance and support. The outcomes, it will be remembered, are:

1 being healthy;
2 staying safe;
3 enjoying and achieving;
4 making a positive contribution; and
5 achieving economic well-being.

(OfSTED, 2005d)

For example, 'the care, advice, guidance and other support provided to safeguard welfare, promote personal development and well-being, and achieve high standards' is considered to relate to outcomes 1, 2 and 3. The evaluation of 'the quality and accessibility of information, advice and guidance to learners in relation to courses and programmes, and, where applicable, to career progression' is related to outcomes 3 and 5.

Guidance on the evaluation of provision gives a further indication of its elements. Good quality care for pupils is exemplified in the 'high level of commitment of staff and their competence in promoting their health and safety'. Arrangements for safeguarding pupils are 'robust and regularly reviewed, and risk assessments are carefully attended to'. In the safe and supportive environment, learners are 'well informed about their future options'. Pupils at risk are 'identified early and effective arrangements put in place to keep them engaged'. The school 'works well with parents and other agencies to ensure that learners make good progress'. (OfSTED, 2005b: 10).

The document, *Conducting the Inspection* (OfSTED, 2005d), conveys an expectation that the school and others comply with statutory guidance in connection with health and safety, child protection and the appointment of staff and any non-compliance is investigated, as a priority. Child protection arrangements are evaluated on all inspections through examining the extent to which the school complies with agreed local area procedures. Also evaluated are: 'whether a child protection officer (CPO) is appointed and adequately trained; whether staff are sufficiently aware of the child protection arrangements; the adequacy of the school's record keeping; the effectiveness of the links with outside agencies; and whether the school's arrangements are adequately reviewed' (ibid.: 15).

Other aspects that a special school may wish to review which relate to self-evaluation include ensuring that learners feel safe from forms of harassment, are confident in approaching staff if troubled and whether they are aware of risks. Is the school providing a safe environment, for example reflected in the state of repair of accommodation and equipment and how well pupils are taught to use equipment safely? (see ibid.: 15). Records of pupil exclusions and reasons for pupils persistently not attending may give indications of whether a school is and is felt to be a safe environment. Where attendance of pupils is poor, or where they are excluded or 'drop out in significant numbers', how does the school attempt to re-engage them? (see ibid.: 15). The monitoring of the progress of learners, how well they are supported, whether they know their targets and whether these are sufficiently challenging are evaluated. The quality of guidance is indicated by such aspects as 'the

---

Box 5.3 TOR VIEW SCHOOL, LANCASHIRE

Tor View School, Rossendale, Lancashire is a co-educational day community special school for 114 pupils aged 4 to 19 years having moderate, severe, or profound and multiple learning difficulties. The school has an intensive support centre for pupils with severe challenging behaviour. Many staff have advanced qualifications in providing for pupils with learning difficulties; speech and language difficulties; medical needs and physical difficulties.

The school day is extended through after-school and weekend activities open to all families in the areas who have children with special educational needs; and a holiday play and activity programme. Each pupil has a designated teacher responsible for their welfare and to ensure they are achieving and happy in the school. This named teacher is responsible for forming the pupil's progress file and the 'passport to progress' and coordinating the pupil's annual school review. A weekly achievement assembly, to which all parents are invited, celebrates success in and out of school.

In ensuring the well-being of pupils, the school encourages the extensive involvement of a range of professionals including speech and language therapists, occupational therapists and physiotherapists. Pupils' views are listened to carefully and older pupils receive clear guidance on their future choices. Parents and pupils are fully involved in setting targets and reviewing progress and pupil involvement is increased through advocacy work, transition views and a school council. To help protect them out of school, pupils learn about road safety, cycling and independent travel. Tor View has also achieved the Healthy Schools Award.

quality of information provided to help learners make educational and curriculum choices' as well as the figures indicating the retention rates of pupils on post 16 courses (ibid.: 15). The school's links with other agencies to support learners is also evaluated (ibid.: 16). (See, for example, Box 5.3.)

Some implications

Child protection arrangements need to conform to locally agreed procedures, which, among other aims, seek to coordinate the work of different agencies. Principles include that due consideration is given to the views of pupils and parents and to contextual matters such as the pupil's religion, race, culture and linguistic background. The school may intervene to protect a pupil from harm where necessary. It follows that staff should know situations in which steps may be taken, for example staff need to know signs of possible abuse and procedures to follow. Also, it is important that special school staff are aware of groups of pupils who may be particularly vulnerable, for example children in local authority care, and pupils requiring special medical or dietary requirements. The formation of Local Safeguarding Children Boards is linked under the Children Act 2004 to a duty on key partners to take part.

The school should have arrangements in place to ensure that each pupil is well known to at least one member of staff. It should actively promote healthy and safe living. Aspects of providing a safe environment include arrangements to ensure appropriate management of access to the Internet including access for pupils who board at school. The hygienic disposal of waste, practices when pupils are off the school site, and safe procedures for lifting pupils are among other considerations.

Guidance and support in relation to academic achievement and personal development are related to the monitoring of these. Pupils should have access to well-informed support, advice and guidance as they progress through school, for example from a teacher or mentor. Effective induction procedures should be in place, for example for new pupils and for pupils transferring to different school phases. For older pupils, guidance and support includes that relating to career choices and information, work-related experience, information and guidance about training, further education and employment. In England, the contribution of the Connexions Personal Adviser can be valuable, although it is important that Connexions Advisers are fully aware of the special educational needs of pupils and their possible implications.

Special schools respond in different ways to the implication of providing good quality care, guidance and support. For example Barrs Court School, Hereford makes it clear in its prospectus that special procedures may have to be followed to keep children safe.

Where care and health and safety involves medical care and personal care of pupils, again there are particular implications that a special school will want to develop to ensure that the best provision is made.

Box 5.4 BARRS COURT SCHOOL, HEREFORDSHIRE

The prospectus for Barrs Court School, Herefordshire states:

> it is often the case that a child who has disabilities is unable to make disclosures about offences committed against them because of their limited abilities to communicate messages and/or to understand the nature of the offence committed against them.
>
> (Barrs Court School Prospectus 2004–5: 23)

The point is made that,

> Because some pupils are unable to provide verbal or written disclosures, it is sometimes necessary to note any sudden changes in the pupil's behaviour and/or appearance that cannot be readily explained. Should there be any evidence that these changes may be linked to a child protection issue then the school will follow the child protection guidelines as if the pupil concerned had made a direct disclosure.
>
> (ibid.: 23)

The quality and accessibility of information, advice and guidance to learners regarding courses, programmes and career progression has to be particularly carefully thought through in some special schools where the pupils may have difficulties expressing preferences. Long-term work involving encouraging choices, decision making, schools councils, advocacy services and the close involvement of parents can all contribute to dealing with such difficulties.

Thinking points

Readers may wish to consider:

*   the school's provision in the light of Every Child Matters outcomes;
*   the school's understanding of care, guidance and support ensuring that it complements any guidance that is given locally and nationally;
*   steps taken to regularly review and improve provision in this area.

Key texts

OfSTED (2005a) *Every Child Matters: Framework for the Inspection of Schools in England from September 2005* (HMI 2435), London, OfSTED.

HM Government (2006) *Working Together to Safeguard Children: A Guide to Interagency Working to Safeguard and Promote the Welfare of Children* (www.everychildmatters. gov.uk/socialcare/safeguarding/workingtogether).

This guidance sets out how individuals and organisations should work together to safeguard children, especially those who may be vulnerable, and promote their welfare.

Digging

Chapter 6

Ambitious target setting

Target setting can help raise standards, offers a benchmark of progress, can demonstrate underperformance in a cohort or across a curriculum area, provides evidence for the school's governing body and supports accountability.

This chapter examines diagnostic and curriculum-based assessments and the way they inform assessments made when teaching; accreditation as a form of assessment and links between assessment and teaching as indicated in the OfSTED framework. The chapter briefly considers recording and reporting. I then outline some features of target setting, in particular how Individual Education Plan (IEP) targets and cohort targets can inform one another, before touching on benchmarking and value added in the special school.

Aspects of assessment

The Assessment Reform Group suggested several factors through which assessment can be improved: effective feedback to pupils; pupils being actively involved in their learning; fine-tuning teaching to take account of the results of assessment; recognising the powerful impact of assessment on pupils' motivation and self-esteem; and pupils being able to assess themselves and understand how they can improve (Assessment Reform Group, 1999: 15). Approaches to assessment are now considered in which these points may be borne in mind.

Diagnostic assessment

Diagnostic assessment, involving finding out what a child knows and how he learns, may begin with assessment information from the pupil's previous school. Diagnostic assessments and related advice and support are of course provided by a range of professionals including the educational psychologist, speech and language therapist, occupational therapist, audiologist, physiotherapist and so on. The special school will also use its own assessments, including standardised tests.

Assessments about how the pupil learns may draw on professional experience of how pupils with particular types of SEN tend to learn. For example, the school will take into consideration that pupils with autism tend to benefit from signals to indicate when transitions, such as changes of activity, are about to take place and from a visual timetable. These generalised professional judgements will be modified in the light of how a particular pupil does in fact learn.

Such assessments help build a picture of weakness and strengths in learning relating to the pupil's SEN. For a pupil with behavioural, emotional and social difficulties, assessments of social skills or of aspects of self-esteem may be a particular focus; while for a child experiencing communication difficulties a particularly detailed assessment of phonological skills, or semantic or pragmatic skills may be especially relevant.

One purpose of such assessments is to help ensure the suitability of the approaches to teaching and learning. If the pupil is considered to have dyslexia and assessments indicate a particular difficulty with visual processing including visual tracking, the teacher will be careful to ensure that strategies are in place to reduce its impact. These might include reducing the occasions when it is necessary for the pupil to translate writing from a white- or blackboard to a workbook; using instead worksheets with the information on the desk beside the pupil's own workbook and where further strategies would be of benefit, such as using different colours for each line.

Curriculum-based assessments

Curriculum-based assessments may relate to the National Curriculum (NC) including measures of progress for pupils working towards level 1 of the NC. These include performance indicator scales (P scales), Performance Indicators for Value Added Target Setting (PIVATS), B Squared and EQUALS. Schools, for example St Margaret's School, The Children's Trust, Surrey (www.thechildrenstrust.org.uk), have developed their own detailed forms of assessment particularly for recognising progress below level 1 of the NC (Farrell, 2006f: 9). The relevance of curriculum-based assessment underlines the importance of the curriculum itself.

The curriculum in a special school is designed according to what it is judged the pupil needs to learn and how the child learns. A curriculum for pupils with moderate learning difficulties may cover NC programmes of study but may be distinctive in its emphasis on practical and experiential ways of learning (Farrell, 2006b: ch. 2). One for learners with profound and multiple learning difficulties will draw much more on developmental underpinnings of learning (Farrell, 2006b: ch. 5). The range and variety of experiences offered and opportunities to develop skills will provide the opportunities for assessment that sample them. Curriculum-based assessment is dependent on the curriculum for what it can assess, and opportunities for assessment built into planning emerge because of the way the curriculum and programmes of work are designed.

Assessment and teaching

The document *Planning, Teaching and Assessing the Curriculum for Pupils with Learning Difficulties: General Guidelines* (DfEE/QCA, 2001) suggests that effective assessment and record keeping can be supported by various features including 'specifying time for observation in a unit of work' and 'targeting specific pupils for observation and recording in particular lessons, ensuring that all learners are assessed in all subjects over time' (p. 24).

Such assessments can be effectively shared with the learners to indicate the next steps and how he or she can improve.

By combining data from diagnostic and curriculum-based assessment the school can begin to make a professional judgement about the pupil's likely progress. Assessment in teaching and learning is therefore a dynamic process. It builds on previous diagnostic assessments to inform its approach, the use of resources, pace and other features of teaching and learning. Teaching also draws on curriculum-related assessments to help determine the content of teaching and its direction. From these two sources and from the response of the pupils, the teacher assesses the pupil's understanding and emerging skills and uses this ongoing assessment to further modify teaching.

Accreditation as a form of assessment

Accreditation concerns the formal acknowledgement and recording of the attainments of pupils. Reaching those attainments has to be challenging for the pupil, but the special school will also take care to ensure that its accreditation provides opportunities for pupils to show what they can do. This often means that accreditation is based on coursework and regular assessment evidence.

Accreditation also conveys the pupil's attainments to parents, potential employers, college admissions officers and others, making it important that the form of accreditation is widely known and understood. Pupils' accreditation is also important to the school as the results contribute towards the school's value added scores. Some forms of accreditation used by special schools such as Award Scheme Development Accreditation Network (ASDAN), the National Skills Profile, and Entry Level certificates may not be well known locally. The special school may therefore seek to raise the profile of the accreditation and help local employers and others recognise the level of attainment it represents. Organising information workshops for local employers may assist this. Where a special school has a local employer as a member of the governing body, the governor may use local networks to help ensure other employers' awareness is raised.

Links between other assessments used in special schools and accreditation help ensure accreditation is at a suitable level. This may be reflected in a smooth gradation from the curriculum schemes of work related to the school's assessments to the programmes associated with national accreditation. More specifically, the special school may seek a gradation from its curriculum and assessment for lower, middle and higher attainers in a subject or curriculum area to the different levels of national accreditation. This does preclude any particular pupil progressing more rapidly than anticipated (because of conservative predictions or particularly effective teaching and learning), or more slowly than expected (for example because of absence or illness) and subsequently transferring to programmes leading to different levels of accreditation.

A National Skills Profile and portfolio provide a means of formative assessment leading to a description of what the pupil can do. Main aspects of former Records of Achievement that also appear to apply to Profiles have been well described some years ago and are: that they imply assessment is a continuing process; that they recognise only success providing evidence rather than judgement; that they suggest that all experiences are important; that they are participative and are considered to enhance learning; and that they are owned by the pupil (Lawson, 1996).

Assessment and the OfSTED framework

Inspectors' evaluation of teaching and learning (OfSTED, 2005a) includes evaluating 'the suitability and rigour of assessment in planning and monitoring learners' progress' (ibid.: 19). This is further elaborated in guidance to inspectors of schools (OfSTED, 2005b). Among the characteristics of good teaching is that, 'Based on thorough and accurate assessment that informs learners how to improve, work is closely tailored to the full range of learners' needs, so that all can succeed. Learners are guided to assess their work themselves' (ibid.: 8).

Assessment informs planning to the extent that it indicates the level at which a pupil is working and the likely next steps. This feeds into short-term planning so that what a pupil has already learned and can do is used as a basis for what he might learn next. Assessment informs the monitoring of their progress because it enables the teacher to track what the pupil is achieving in relation to what it was expected he should be able to subsequently do. In all this, teachers can help and encourage pupils to make assessments of the pupil's performance.

Recording and reporting

Recording assessment outcomes involves having routines and procedures in the school and allocating sufficient time for systematic recording. Diagnostic assessment of individual pupils may be recorded together with those of other pupils forming a profile of cohorts of pupils within the school, for example lower, middle and higher attainers. Assessments highlighting strengths and weakness, often recorded in IEPs, may inform the approach to lessons. Curriculum-based assessment may be recorded on curriculum documents or lesson plans or using grids including pupils' names and the knowledge and skills to be achieved.

Records may include:

- extracts from curriculum plans (as records of experience);
- comments about pupil responses;
- annotated samples of work;
- photographs, or tape or video sequences;
- pupil self-assessment and peer recordings;
- a pupil's record of achievement or progress file; and
- assessments related to external accreditation.

(DfEE/QCA, 2001: 26)

The school will also be likely to have systems and procedures for the whole school moderation of assessments aimed at improving their reliability. Where sufficient time is allocated for this process, it can act as a confirmation of judgements, an indication that judgements were over- or under-optimistic (and possibly why) and can act as an important induction into judging standards for new staff.

Reporting the outcomes of assessment involves establishing the purpose of the reporting and for whom it is made, for example, informing parents and others of progress at an annual review of the pupil's statement. Reporting draws together information from various sources and gathered over a period of time, presenting it clearly and briefly so that the audience are confident the information is reliable and useful. Surveys of parents' views on the usefulness of school reports may indicate areas for improvement, helping the school refine its practice.

Target setting

The work of The Royal School for the Deaf and Communication Disorders, Cheshire illustrates some of the important relationships between assessment and target setting (see Box 6.1).

Individual pupils and cohorts

Aids to ensuring that sufficient progress is made for pupils with SEN include setting individual targets relating to progress through IEPs, and progress targets set for cohorts of pupils including statutorily required whole school

Box 6.1 THE ROYAL SCHOOL FOR THE DEAF AND COMMUNICATION DISORDERS, CHESHIRE

The Royal School for the Deaf and Communication Disorders, (www.rds manchester.org) Cheadle, Cheshire is a non-maintained co-educational day and boarding school and college for 75 pupils aged 7 to 21 years. Accredited by the DfES, it has accommodation for 60 boarders from the age of 8 for up to 52 weeks per year. Students have communication difficulties arising from sensory loss, severe learning difficulties, and autistic spectrum disorders or challenging behaviour.

For assessment purposes, the school uses P levels, pre-entry levels and PIVATS for English/communication, mathematics, science, and personal and social development. In the school, P levels are also used to assess all foundation subjects. Assessment levels are included in the pupil's individual education plan, annual review reports and information for subject leaders.

The school places great value on target setting for individuals so that relevant teaching is provided to match the requirements of each learner. The school has developed a simple tracking system so that progress can be analysed for each learner over time.

Class targets for small groups of pupils over a year have been set at performance review and development meetings and are related to whole school targets and initiatives. Curriculum subject leaders are starting to look at assessment results in their subject areas as part of their self-evaluation and to inform curriculum development.

Whole school target setting allows the comparison of assessment results against different criteria, for example, students who have autism/multi-sensory impairment; subjects; or areas within a subject, such as space, shape and measures in mathematics. Students are assessed at the beginning of a Key Stage and then a target is projected for the end of the Key Stage.

The school has found that as pupils vary from year to year, it is more meaningful to make sub-groups and set targets for students taking into account their current achievement. Moderation is considered paramount.

performance targets. (Independent special schools do not have a statutory duty to set performance targets although many do so.) Although tension exists between individual and cohort targets, it is important they are considered in relation to one another with the school seeking to identify areas for improvement using discretion and careful professional judgement.

On the face of it, IEPs look as though they would clearly contribute to ensuring progress is as good as can reasonably be expected. They set out targets, which are often agreed with the pupil, as well as delineating strategies to reach those targets and arrangements to evaluate progress. They can also be related to curriculum objectives. Profiles of such assessments can be monitored allowing apparent discrepancies in performance to be investigated and action taken as necessary. For example, the profile of a pupil's progress across different subjects can be examined on the assumption that it would be similar unless substantiated reasons indicated otherwise, for example relating to the characteristics of a particular curriculum subject or type of disability or disorder.

However, IEP targets may be relatively short term and based on what it is thought the individual pupil requires to progress better. Also, it remains difficult to know whether targets are sufficiently challenging. A teacher might claim they are, based on professional experience and knowledge of the pupil. A visitor to the school who sees many pupils with apparently similar types of SEN might question whether the targets are sufficiently stretching, citing knowledge of other schools where pupils seem to do better. Or more precisely, LEA data may suggest underperformance of pupils. So what more can be done to ensure good progress? One approach is the judicial use of cohort target setting.

Cohort target setting

Target setting is a way of setting priorities for the school and its pupils. Assessment data may indicate progress anomalies for different groups – such as boys and girls or different ethnic groups – that may require investigation, and could suggest setting targets to help monitor strategies aimed at rectifying variations in provision. Again, assessment data will indicate progress across different subjects, suggesting areas of underachievement to improve. For example, if a special school finds that, examining its data, progress in handwriting appears slower than expected, it might consider setting targets for developing this. The data would indicate the progress that had been made, say in the previous year. The school would agree on the likely progress expected the following year if similar progress were maintained.

Given that better progress was wanted, the school would make a distinction between predicted levels of achievement and targets. If it was expected that 60 per cent of pupils would progress to a specified level of competence in writing, the target might be that 70 per cent of pupils would make such progress. The target would be more ambitious than the prediction.

To reach the target, given that the school was already presumably doing its best, there would need to be extra provision. This might be extra teaching assistant time spent on teaching writing skills, a new writing scheme, more time in the school timetable for teaching writing or a programme to involve parents in supporting writing along with suitable in-school training. Because writing is a priority, the costs of whatever elements of provision were decided upon would be allocated towards reaching the targets.

Progress towards the targets would be monitored, perhaps termly to see if it was sufficient and adjustments would be made to provision as necessary. Assessments might be made at a fixed point in time. After targets had been set and a time-scale agreed, the pupils would be assessed again say a term later to ascertain if the targets had been reached.

Another approach is to set targets for individual pupils at annual reviews in terms of uniform assessments. It might be decided that all pupils should progress a certain number of steps in P scales in one year. At the annual review, IEP targets would be set and it might be agreed to review them termly. Targets would therefore be in terms of P scale progress for a year ahead. At the end of the year, for each pupil, progress would be noted, and as all pupils moved to their second annual review after targets had been set, it would be seen what proportion had reached the agreed targets. While this approach works for continually expected targets, it does not indicate whether a particular initiative is working.

Guidance on target setting provided by the Department for Education and Employment (DfEE, 2001), whose intended audience included special schools (e.g. ibid.: 10–11, 14–15, 16, 17–18), helpfully included discussion of setting targets for pupils achieving below NC level 1. But unfortunately it loses the useful distinction between predictions and targets, treating them as synonymous (e.g. ibid.: 8).

There are also potential difficulties with using such assessments as P scales too uncritically including that their application may be inconsistent and their moderation difficult. Also, it can be misleading to assume that the breadth of the steps of progress implied in P scales is consistent between different levels of the P scale. Indeed some P levels (P7, P8) are considered by some to be harder to achieve than level 1 of the National Curriculum to which they are supposed to lead.

The challenges posed by cohort size changes, pupil mobility and a special school having a 'generic' population with a range of SEN is indicated by the example of Durham Trinity School, Durham City (see Box 6.2).

Joining individual and cohort approaches to target setting

Setting targets can be particularly effective when the process is an integral part of school self-evaluation and improvement. The analysis of assessment

Box 6.2 DURHAM TRINITY SCHOOL, DURHAM CITY

Durham Trinity School, Durham City is a community special school for 180 boys and girls aged 2 to 19 years having a range of SEN including moderate, severe or profound and multiple learning difficulties; behavioural, emotional and social difficulties; and communication difficulties (CD) including autistic spectrum disorder. The school occupies three sites: one for pupils aged 2 to 12 years; the other two for students aged 11 to 19 years. The school's awards include an Artsmark silver; a sport England activemark gold; and a school achievement award gained in 2002.

The school uses targets for year cohorts required by the DfES but also incorporates its own experience, using targets having currency in the wider community. The school's approach to assessment and target setting involves a two-year cycle (initial target setting, one year on review, and a following year evaluation of targets). Targets are set in relation to main types of SEN: MLD, SLD, BESD, CD, PMLD, and 'SLD with challenging behaviour'. Each year, targets are set in mathematics, English and science for two years ahead, with the target being reviewed after one year.

For example, in mathematics in Key Stage 1, percentages may be set as P scales and National Curriculum levels and the percentages of pupils expected to reach the targets such as: 10 per cent will achieve level 2B; 10 per cent P7; 10 per cent P6; 20 per cent P4; 10 per cent P3 (i); 10 per cent P2 (II); 10 per cent P2 (i); 10 per cent P1 (ii); 10 per cent P1 (i). If these targets were set in 2006, they would be reviewed in 2007 and it would be expected that they would be realised in 2008. Targets in Key Stage 2 tend to be in terms of the percentage of pupils expected to achieve specified National Curriculum levels in mathematics, English and science using teacher assessment. At Key Stage 3, targets are set in terms of mathematics and science tests, and English and ICT teacher assessment.

At Key Stage 4, targets are set for the percentage of students expected to achieve: science Entry Levels 1, 2 and 3; Entry Levels in English, ICT and Enterprise; single entry foundation GCSE; Key Skills Application of Number; the Prince's Trust XL Award (Bronze); ASDAN (Bronze/Silver Challenge, Transition Challenge – two modules or one module); physical education (Junior Sports Leader Award and OCR Entry Level); and food studies (City and Guilds Entry Level 1 Certificate). The school considers secondary level targets being externally marked and accredited adds to the achievement.

Among the challenges the school sees with target setting is that the cohort size changes year on year and with some cohorts being very small, the performance of one pupil can have a significant effect on overall percentages.

Sometimes pupil mobility is a significant and not always predictable factor. Pupils may join the school in September from mainstream, as part of the cohort for whom targets are set but the documentation from their school is often too imprecise to determine achievement level. Because of the school's generic population, year on year cohorts differ making finding a benchmarking partner school with comparative types of SEN and similar base-line achievement difficult. Also, the percentage of targets can differ year on year because of the nature of the cohort and the level of functioning within the group so that it may be unreasonable to expect an increase in the targets for a particular year. For some pupils maintaining a level constitutes significant achievement.

Since 2004, the school has been part of the DfES value-added pilot study and it has become clear that the issues faced are very different from those of mainstream schools. Nevertheless the school has achieved good value added results so far as these can be judged.

data indicates areas to investigate and may suggest action to be taken to rectify anomalies or tackle underperformance. The school improvement plan and the summary of school self-evaluation can reflect and be informed by the school's analysis of its assessment data. Ongoing monitoring of progress allows modifications to be made to provision to help ensure targets are reached.

Target setting often informs performance management and teachers' performance can be linked to improved pupil progress. Governors need to be clear about the purpose of target setting and how they can monitor the process and outcomes. The challenge is to bind individual target setting together with cohort target setting so one informs the other and so individual targets are lifted by wider challenge.

In determining how best to ensure data is interpreted and acted upon, the school's management structure is influential. A school having subject coordinators may make them responsible for initially collecting and analysing subject data. They may then be responsible for working with other teachers. Where a special school has age phase coordinators, these may work with staff to set targets relating to age groups.

Slated Row School, Milton Keynes, provides an example of a school linking target setting, pupil progress and school improvement (see Box 6.3).

Benchmarking and value added

A precursor to effective benchmarking is the moderation of teacher assessments of pupils. This allows staff in a particular special school to compare their assessments with other special schools with pupils of similar ages and types

Box 6.3 SLATED ROW SCHOOL, MILTON KEYNES

Slated Row, Milton Keynes educates up to 160 students aged 4 to 19 years having moderate learning difficulties, some of whom have more complex SEN, and is in the top 15 per cent of all schools nationally for value added. It has a purpose-built technology suite with garage, science laboratory, sixth-form centre, music studio, soft play/therapy room and information and communication technology network base. Partnership between parents and the school is encouraged through home/school books, reading record books, open days, parents' evenings, productions, social events and sporting activities. Pupils' success is celebrated through awards, certificates, good work assemblies, praise, letters home and by displaying work in school.

Slated Row believes that target setting is an integral part of school improvement; that school self-evaluation is a critical component in effective target setting and that pupil progress is at the heart of school improvement. By reviewing school performance and pupil progress the school identifies areas of underachievement and set targets for improvement. Target setting, pupil progress and school improvement are therefore inextricably linked.

The school collates pupil assessment and achievement data over time at individual, cohort and whole school level. Progress for individual pupils and whole cohorts of pupils are tracked, so that over time the school has a clear understanding of the rate of progress that can be expected year on year. Analysing this data forms a basis for evaluating how well pupils are achieving and the overall effectiveness of the school. It also enables a school to demonstrate value added.

Pupil progress is tracked in a number of ways: teacher assessments, end of Key Stage results, individual education plans and through externally accredited courses. In all National Curriculum subjects teachers regularly assess and record pupil progress and annually pupil attainment is formally recorded, reported and shared. Records are kept in individual pupil files which move with them through the school, by the subject coordinators, form tutors and by the curriculum manager, enabling progress to be analysed and tracked at an individual level, in year groups, in subject groups and in Key Stage groups.

At the start of the next academic year, each year group has a target sheet. This sheet records individual pupils' current attainments in English, mathematics and science and has two further columns, one for predicted progress by the end of the academic year and one to record actual progress. Once teachers have filled in the first two columns they are submitted and analysed by the curriculum manager to ensure realistic targets have been set. Targets are discussed with subject coordinators and Key Stage managers as well as all teachers. The curriculum manager/head teacher use this information to set whole school targets across subject areas and cohorts of pupils. School self-evaluation priorities and the school development plan support this process.

At the end of the academic year the third column is filled in and the results analysed. For all pupils who meet or exceed their target (NC level may be the same or 1 level higher), the column is coloured yellow. For pupils who do not achieve their target (but may have moved 1 level) it is coloured orange. In the case of pupils who move 1 NC level it is coloured green and for pupils who move 2 or more levels it is coloured pink. Percentages are then calculated in year groups, key stages or for other combinations of pupils such as girls/boys or ethnic minorities in each of the subjects.

Using colour enables the school to see results in each subject strand, across the whole subject and across year groups, and obvious patterns are apparent where performance is above or below what is expected. These results then enable staff to analyse why performance was not as expected. It may, for example, highlight one subject area where results are below what would normally be expected or, in the primary phase, may indicate a class who are under performing. This may be due to unsatisfactory teaching, staff absence or changes, or simply because the moderation of previous assessments was not robust.

This information is used to set priorities in the school development plan for the next academic year, for example highlighting where training for teachers might be needed, or where assessment needs to be better moderated. It can also indicate where a whole school focus is needed to address pupils' underperformance in, for example speaking and listening skills. Analysis of pupil progress is therefore an integral part of school improvement.

of SEN. While this is done though accreditation meetings for Key Stage 4, it is less apparent for other Key Stages and particular challenges arise in moderating level of attainment for pupils with PMLD (e.g. OfSTED, 2004: 22). DVD exemplars of pupils working at particular levels offer one way of helping develop more effective moderation.

Benchmarking is a way of comparing schools' and pupils' progress to see if the progress in one school is as much as can be reasonably expected. If two schools can agree that they have pupils with broadly similar SEN who are at roughly similar starting points, they may decide to compare their relative progress, over a year. Each might adopt a different strategy to try to improve progress, for example in raising pupils' self-esteem as indicated on an agreed assessment. Each school can therefore support and learn from the other, further strengthening the credibility of the targets set.

The value added by the school is the progress that is achieved over and above that originally expected. Any extra progress will have been achieved by putting in place strategies and resources to reach the targets agreed, and the schools learning from each other as they work together in the bench-marking process.

Some LEAs provide their special schools with data, which is potentially useful in helping the schools be sure that they are maintaining good enough progress. For example, in Hampshire, previous three-year rolling averages of progress achieved in local special schools, differentiated for profound, severe and moderate learning difficulties, give an indication of how an individual special school is performing compared with others.

The Plymouth BARE project (www.recordingandassessment.co.uk) gets its name from the early name of curriculum guidelines developed for pupils performing Below Age Related Expectations. Software covers recording, achievement, target setting, assessment and reporting. P scales, National Curriculum progress to level 5, Foundation Stage Profiles and Foundation Stage stepping-stones are included in an interactive format. P levels and National Curriculum levels are further broken down into sentences for more detailed assessment and individual 'progress charts' show progress through all assessments. Further developments are taking place at the request of teachers, including rewriting the software to provide an online assessment tool and adding additional information to allow regional (south west) benchmarking and links with any national benchmarking data that becomes available (ahemmens@woodlands.plymouth.sch.uk).

The organisation EQUALS (www.equals.co.uk) supports setting targets for pupils working within the P scales. Participating schools submitting their P scale data (English, mathematics, science, personal and social education) to Durham University receive an overview of individual and year group averages compared with other pupils in England. Schools entering data for second and subsequent years receive value added scores for every pupil indicating whether they have made above or below average progress in each subject area. From 2006 schools also receive predicted P level scores for each subject and each pupil for the subsequent year.

Among the challenges faced by any national approach to benchmarking is the diverse nature of pupils in special schools; the different identification and assessment regimes in local authorities, and the differing range of places (for example the degree to which a local authority tends to use pupil referral units for pupils with BESD and the extent to which it uses residential schools outside the local authority).

Thinking points

Readers may wish to consider:

- how the effectiveness of their school's assessment procedures may be improved;
- how their school's approach to individual target setting can be improved;
- whether their school's arrangements for benchmarking and value added measures are robust enough;
- the extent to which individual and cohort target setting can be dovetailed together.

Key resources

DfEE/QCA (2001) *Planning, Teaching and Assessing the Curriculum for Pupils with Learning Difficulties: General Guidelines*, London, DfEE/QCA, 2001.

In the QCA website (www.qca.org.uk/14-19) follow indications to 'special schools' for a few examples of special schools' organisation of their Key Stage 4 curriculum including accreditation.

Drawing

Chapter 7

Confident multi-professional working

This chapter examines aspects of multi-professional working looking at its nature and interrelationships with multi-agency working. The challenges and possible success factors of multi-professional working are outlined. Legislation and regulations aimed at encouraging cooperation are touched on.

The importance of multi-level leadership of governors and senior managers is considered and related OfSTED guidance is elaborated. Multi-professional working in the special school is indicated through looking at day-to-day practice; assessment and the Common Assessment Framework; and liaison. (See, for example, Box 7.1.)

The nature of multi-professional working

By multi-professional working in the present context, I mean professionals with different perspectives and backgrounds working together successfully as a team or in a wider structure on a common enterprise of day-to-day practice, assessment or liaison for the benefit of pupils with SEN.

The range of professionals is wide and includes teachers, specialist teachers for example of children with visual or hearing impairments, audiologists, learning support assistants, speech and language therapists, occupational therapists, physiotherapists, arts therapists (art, drama, dance/movement, music), play therapists, mobility teachers, 'conductors', prosthetists, educational and clinical psychologists, general practitioners, psychiatrists, counsellors, psychotherapists, paediatricians, orthoptists, orthopaedic surgeons, nurses, social workers, dieticians, portage workers, support workers from voluntary bodies, educational welfare officers and others.

Multi-agency working and multi-professional working

I am taking multi-agency working to mean professionals employed by different agencies working together effectively. The agencies may be education services, social care services, health services or youth justice services. By multi-professional working, as suggested in the previous section, I mean professionals

---

Box 7.1 ST PIERS SCHOOL, THE NCYPE, LINGFIELD, SURREY

Multi-professional working

St Piers School, Lingfield, Surrey (www.ncype.org.uk), a non-maintained special school, is part of the provision of The National Centre for Young People with Epilepsy (NCYPE), which is the UK's major provider of specialist services for children and young people with epilepsy and other special needs. As well as St Piers School for children aged 5 to 16 years, there is a sixth form; a further education college for students aged 16 to 25 years; and a National Epilepsy Outreach, Assessment and Rehabilitation Service. A range of hostels and houses across the site accommodate groups of 6 to 12 students.

Multi-professional working is strongly emphasised. The NCYPE staff of 600 includes teachers, teaching assistants, residential social workers, paediatric neurologists, nurses, therapists, psychiatrists, Connexions personal advisers and psychologists. The NCYPE multi-professional assessment service is provided to young people across the UK. A three-day diagnostic assessment involves electroencephalogram telemetry (recording brain activity) and input from nursing and psychological staff. The interdisciplinary assessment provides detailed diagnostic information and evaluation of the impact of epilepsy on personal, social and educational skills and the implications for education and support. The length and type of assessment is planned individually. Rehabilitation, outreach services and training packages are also offered.

---

from different disciplines working together. These may be a medical nurse, a medical doctor and a physiotherapist all working for the health services. A teacher, an educational psychologist and a teaching assistant may work together, all employed by the education service. But an extra challenge is posed when members of staff from different professional backgrounds are also employed by different agencies and seek to work together. This means that multi-professional working can refer to professionals employed by the same service working together or professionals employed by different services working together.

Multi-agency working has been related to three service delivery models (DfES, 2005b: ch. 2). First, a multi-agency panel might meet periodically, perhaps monthly. In the second model, members of different services might be seconded to a multi-agency team either part-time or full-time, an example being a behaviour support team. The third model involves integrated services working in a common location and with a common philosophy. One way of contributing to this third model is through extended schools or full service schools or children's centres.

Special schools can be well placed to initiate and develop integrated services, and there are examples of good and developing practice in this area. Such developments can lead to better communication between services because of their shared base; opportunities for training together; and a more holistic approach to the child.

Challenges and success factors

Yet what would appear to be basic cooperation, never mind close partnership, has in the past proved elusive. A lack of joint working was reported between services supporting single mothers with children having learning difficulties (Middleton, 1998) and communication between agencies in relation to requirements of the *Special Educational Needs Code of Practice* (DfES, 2001a) have been found wanting (Dyson, Lyn and Millward, 1998). The death of a young girl who was abused and killed by her great aunt and the man with whom they lived, a factor leading to the Every Child Matters programme and other developments in England (www.everychildmatters.gov.uk/ information/), tragically indicates that inter-agency working still has some way to go.

Among the well-rehearsed difficulties relating to multi-disciplinary working in England (or 'challenges' as they are often called in upbeat management speak) are that:

- education and social services are locally organised and funded while the health service has a more direct link to national government;
- geographical boundaries covered by different services are not always coterminous;
- management structures, educational background, perspectives, priorities and salaries are different;
- notions of confidentiality where information ought to be shared are sometimes over-precious; and
- petty power struggles can hinder partnership.

Research into multi-agency working has suggested potential benefits that are summarised elsewhere (DfES, 2005b: ch. 3) and include improvement relating to outcomes for children and families; benefits for staff and services; and providing what children and young people and families say they want.

Given the challenges, success factors for multi-agency working have been suggested and can be considered under four headings: strategic; operational; community and voluntary sector involvement; and evaluation.

Strategic aspects include shared goals and common targets; adequate 'lead-in times'; suitable oversight and accountability regarding the different partnership arrangements (Children's Trusts it is hoped may contribute to this); coterminous administrative boundaries; and good baseline and monitoring data.

Operational features embrace having a clear purpose; roles being clearly defined; developing pay and conditions to be comparable to those carrying out similar work in statutory agencies; joint training; a clear line management structure; recognition of multi-agency skills; partnership agreements; and suitable referral systems and information exchange systems.

Strategies to encourage community and voluntary sector involvement include avoiding procedures that might get in the way of such involvement such as the voluntary body not having enough money, capacity or technical skills to contribute effectively or the other services not sufficiently recognising the contribution the voluntary sector can make.

Evaluation brings in collaboration; using a range of methods of evaluation that are suitable to the task; and good coordination (DfES, 2005b: ch. 4).

Legislation and regulations intended to encourage cooperation

The move towards Children's Authorities is thought to be a positive step that might allow and encourage services to work towards common aims. Under the Children Act 2004 various duties were placed on local authorities. By 2008 all local authorities should appoint a director of children's services and a lead member/councillor; and should have set up a children's trust to encourage interagency cooperation (www.standards.dfes.gov.uk/la/). Also, local authorities must cooperate with other bodies including the health services and the police and private and voluntary organisations to improve outcomes for children. They must set up local safeguarding children boards.

Regulations were developed requiring that, instead of various plans, a single plan be required by 2006 covering the functions of the local authority regarding education and social services for children.

Joint area reviews of children's services are another aspect of this approach (Steering Group for the Inspection of Children's Services, 2004). These reviews are intended to include all services for children and young people ages 0 to 19 years whether from statutory, voluntary or private providers where they receive public funds. While there is flexibility in the remit of the review to respond to particular circumstances, two groups are considered in every review: looked after children; and children and young people with learning difficulties/disabilities. The reviews look at Every Child Matters outcomes across services (replacing former separate education and social care inspections). See also Chapter 5, 'Better children's well-being' in this volume.

Governance, leadership and management: bringing them together

While they may be considered separately, governance, leadership and management are intimately related, I suggest particularly through the feature of leadership.

Governance and leadership

Governors are not responsible for the day-to-day working of the school in a detailed sense but do have broader responsibilities for moulding the vision and setting the direction of the school. The emphasis therefore is on governance itself and on leadership, although aspects sometimes described as management are also involved.

For example, key aspects of governance are vision and strategic direction. The vision of the school might include that it is a 'listening school' that seeks to be aware and respond to the views of pupils, parents and others. Vision statements can seem painfully trite. It would be difficult to envisage governors developing a mission statement saying that they were striving to become a school that does not listen to anyone. But the important point is that such statements are developed into actions that exemplify the vision and are acted upon in the school's daily life.

The strategic framework involves:

- setting aims and objectives for the school;
- adopting policies for achieving those aims and objectives; and
- setting targets for achieving those aims and objectives.

(DfES, 2004a: ch. 4 para. 8)

At a school with a delegated budget, the governing body has a general responsibility for the conduct of the school 'with a view to promoting high standards of educational achievement' (DfES, 2004a: ch. 4, para. 4). The powers and duties of the governing body, as set out in government guidance to governors (e.g. DfES, 2004a; DfES, 2004b), include the following:

- 'Setting appropriate targets for pupil achievement at Key Stages 2, 3 and 4';
- 'Managing the school's budget . . . including determining the staff complement and making decisions on staff pay';
- 'making sure that the curriculum for the school is balanced and broadly based and in particular that the curriculum includes the National Curriculum, religious education and (in secondary schools) sex education';
- 'reporting National Curriculum assessments and examination results to parents, the LEA and to the Department';

- 'appointing the head teacher and deputy head teacher, determining how the appointment of other staff will be managed and establishing procedures for the management of staff conduct and discipline and staff grievances';
- 'establishing, following consultation with all staff, and reviewing annually a performance management policy for staff appraisal';
- 'managing governors' duties to pupils with Special Educational Needs'; and
- 'drawing up an action plan after an inspection'.

(DfES, 2004a: ch. 4, para. 4)

Given these strategic and statutory responsibilities, it is important that governors know the relative strengths and weaknesses of the school for knowing these will help determine the strategic direction of the school, which must be in part to build on its strengths and to rectify as far as possible its weaknesses. In order for governors to securely know the school's strengths and weaknesses there should be procedures to ensure that they know them. In other words, there should be a clear answer to the question, *'how* do governors know the school's strengths and weaknesses?' In part, this relates to the quality and timeliness of information, including information about standards of pupils' achievement to which governors have access. Such information enables the governing body to effectively act as a critical friend.

Leadership and management In the school

Leaders and managers in the school include the head teacher, members of the senior management team and any others with leadership and management responsibility.

In a broad sense, it is important that in leadership and management, these staff members are clear about what it is they are seeking to achieve and how they will achieve it with a central focus on raising the achievement of pupils. Particular strategies may be developed, for example of consultation, decision-making, accountability and so on. The importance of good communication needs to be borne in mind including what is to be communicated, why, how and to what effect. Such elements contribute to the school having a clear sense of direction and are a powerful motivating and team-building force for all.

Strategic planning will include elements such as the allocation of resources and the performance management of staff.

Linked closely to this, operational planning, for example indicated by the school improvement plan, will be developed in consultation with all involved. It will include ensuring the further development of key areas of school life including pupil achievement and well-being; the curriculum; teaching and learning; and care, guidance and support. It will be focused on priorities and will be as simple as possible while conveying clearly what is to be done and how.

Informing all this and being informed by it is the school's process of self-evaluation. This includes monitoring performance data and determining why pupil achievement is as it is. It relates to the process of performance management. It brings in staff recruitment, induction and deployment, monitoring of workload, team working and arrangements, and continuing professional development.

Resource management includes the management of financial resources and a key point is how the school knows whether its financial management is effective or not. This relates to what financial data it has, how it uses this information, and the procedures it follows and how they are monitored. The school should be able to demonstrate that in its management of finances, its dealings are related to raising standards. Judgements about the value for

---

Box 7.2 HOLYPORT MANOR SCHOOL, BERKSHIRE

Holyport Manor School, Maidenhead, Berkshire is a generic special school educating 160 pupils aged 2 to 19 years. All pupils are taught in age-appropriate groups irrespective of the level or complexity of need. The school has a term-time weekday residential unit for up to 28 young people.

Prior to, or as soon as possible near admission, new pupils' parents are offered a meeting to discuss medical history and previous school experiences with professionals working at Holyport Manor. Class teacher and specialist support assistant also attend. The positive feedback these meetings provided from staff and parents led to a whole school training day intended to raise awareness of professionals in school, their roles and how they work as a team. The training day was planned by professionals working in school. It involved providing an introduction to each therapist/specialist and their role. These included speech and language therapist; occupational therapist; physiotherapist; hearing impairment teacher; visual impairment teacher; eating, drinking and swallowing specialist; educational psychologist; and the advanced skills teacher for autism and social communication disorders. In addition, the day involved presenting two case studies of students at Holyport Manor, showing how the different professionals/specialists worked as a team; and workshops conducted by each professional/specialist.

An evaluation of the training day confirmed that it was successful. Workshop numbers were limited so more workshops were requested possibly using twilight sessions. It became clear that induction training needed reviewing. On a practical note, a child psychotherapist joined the team after this training day and the school therefore has to update staff on her role.

money that a school provides is related to the effectiveness of the school balanced against its costs. (See, for example, Box 7.2.)

OfSTED guidance

The document *Every Child Matters: Framework for the Inspection of Schools in England from September 2005* (OfSTED, 2005a: 20–1) refers to the evaluation of leadership and management in raising achievement and supporting all learners. In relation to this inspectors evaluate:

- how effectively performance is monitored and improved through quality assurance and self-assessment;
- how effectively leaders and managers at all levels clearly direct improvement and promote the well-being of learners through high-quality care, education and training;
- how well equality of opportunity is promoted and discrimination tackled so that all learners achieve their potential;
- the adequacy and suitability of staff, including the effectiveness of processes for recruitment and selection of staff to ensure that learners are well taught and protected;
- the adequacy and suitability of specialist equipment, learning resources and accommodation; and
- how effectively and efficiently resources are deployed to achieve value for money.

Where appropriate, inspectors also evaluate:

- how effective are the links made with other providers, services, employers and other organisations to promote the integration of care, education and any extended services to enhance learning and to promote well-being; and
- the effectiveness with which governors and other supervisory boards discharge their responsibilities.

A related document *Using the Evaluation Schedule: Guidance for Inspectors of Schools* (OfSTED, 2005b: 12) describes 'good' leadership and management, which include governance:

> The leadership of the school is successfully focused on raising standards and promoting the personal development and well-being of learners. It has created a common sense of purpose among staff. Through its effective self-evaluation, which takes into account the views of all major stakeholders, managers have a good understanding of the school's strengths and weaknesses and have a good track record of making improvements,

including dealing with any issues from the last inspection. The inclusion of all learners is central to its vision and it is effective in pursuing this and dismantling barriers to engagement. The school runs smoothly on a day-to-day basis. Resources are well used, including any extended services, to improve learners' outcomes and to secure good value for money. Vetting procedures for all adults who work with learners are robust. Good links exist with parents and outside agencies to support its work. The impact is seen in the good progress made by most learners on most fronts, in their sense of security and well-being, and in its deservedly good reputation locally. The leadership and management provide the school with a good capacity to improve.

In a further document, *Conducting the Inspection: Guidance for Inspectors of Schools* (OfSTED, 2005d: 16), other examples and evidence of leadership and management are provided. It is made clear that the judgements apply to the effectiveness of the head teacher, the senior management team and other layers of management. Among the indications of the quality of leadership and management are its impact on the progress, personal development and well-being of learners and the quality of teaching, curriculum and care. In other words the quality of the elements of the framework for inspection are indications of the quality of leadership and management.

Other indications are 'the extent to which the school reaches challenging targets' and the school's recent improvement. Also important are 'the rigour of the school's self-evaluation', its development planning, and evidence of how it has built on its strengths and tackled weaknesses. An indication of how well managers know the school and action taken to improve it is considered to be the 'quality of professional development arrangements'. Evaluations of governance are informed by investigating how effectively 'governors hold the school to account and ensure compliance with legal requirements'.

Linking governance, leadership and management

The governance, leadership and management of a special school should ideally combine to create a clear sense of where the school is going and equally clear methods of how to get there. Governance and leadership are largely to do with direction, while management concerns the most efficient way to proceed. Governors of a school exercise the functions of governance and leadership (although aspects of their role are described as management, for example, 'Managing the school's budget . . . including determining the staff complement and making decisions on staff pay' (DfES, 2004a: ch. 4, para. 4).

The head teacher, senior management team and other school staff with responsibilities exert in varying degrees leadership and management. The common factor is leadership and it is important that the governors and the head teacher are at one about where the school is and where it should go. If this can be achieved, much of the ground is laid to make governance, leadership and management coherent.

Multi-disciplinary working in the special school

Earlier, I referred to multi-disciplinary working as involving professionals working together successfully as a team or in a wider structure on a common enterprise of day-to-day practice, assessment and liaison for the benefit of pupils with SEN. Examples of good multi-disciplinary day-to-day practice, assessment and liaison can be readily found in many special schools.

Special schools seem often able to tackle many of the hindrances cited earlier. For example, special schools may employ a professional such as a speech and language therapist who is usually employed directly by the health services. This can help create a more cohesive team although arrangements may need to be made for support and supervision of the therapist's work. Where a wide range of professionals meet in the special school, the different geographical boundaries of their managers is of less importance because the focus is on direct work with pupils. Also, where staff regularly meet and work together, issues of confidentiality can be agreed and power struggles perhaps more readily recognised and resolved. (See, for example, Box 7.3 on p. 96).

Day-to-day practice

The opportunities to develop close multi-professional working in a special school are extensive. For example, with regard to practice, or the day-to-day working with children and young people, special schools bring together many professionals to do just this.

The teacher and learning support assistant work with the physiotherapist on jointly developed programmes of physical development that are jointly assessed. The speech and language therapist works with the teacher and learning support assistant to develop language intervention, which the speech and language therapist may then oversee or directly contribute to. Residential social workers communicate regularly and comprehensively with teachers and others to ensure that the aim of providing a 24-hour curriculum is more closely realised. In hospital schools and schools which educate pupils with medical needs, medical staff including doctors, nurses and others may work full-time on the special school site to provide continuity of care alongside education.

Where different professionals see pupils individually but in the same special school, there are regular and important opportunities for informal as well as more formal liaison. For example in Chelfham Mill School (www.chelfhammillschool.co.uk) in Devon, staff include members of the

Box 7.3 EXHALL GRANGE SCHOOL AND SCIENCE COLLEGE

Multi-professional working

Exhall Grange School and Science College (EGSSC), Coventry, maintained by Warwickshire LEA, educates 200 boys and girls aged 2 to 19 years having various SEN including visual impairment; physical disability; communication difficulties; behavioural, emotional and social difficulties; and autistic spectrum disorder. Pupils who are admitted are attaining or expected to attain within age average expectations although the nursery educates children with profound and multiple learning difficulties who later usually go on to other special schools. EGSSC's awards include a Sports Mark Gold Award and a School Achievement Award. It is a specialist school and has applied to become a children's centre. Several staff have a mandatory qualification in visual impairment.

EGSSC's multi-professional working relates to its existing roles and its aspirations for extended provision, developing as a children's centre. For example, an early years assessment centre has multi-disciplinary staff of a speech and language therapist, physiotherapist, mobility officer, occupational therapist, educational psychologist, advisory teacher of the visually impaired and hearing impaired, dietician and medical staff. The site includes SEN support services in the form of the Disability Inclusion Sensory and Communication Service. The provision also has a full-time physiotherapy department staffed by physiotherapists from the Nuneaton Hospital Trust and a healthcare base for paediatric therapies and community nursing support on site.

EGSSC is developing extended provision including negotiating a contract for a voluntary organisation, 'Take a Break', to offer out-of-hours facilities on the site and developing the range of services offered on the campus. It has scheduled development as a children's centre in the period 2006 to 2008. The intention is to work with the local education and social care services, the health service and voluntary bodies to offer holistic child provision and 'one stop' centre for parents wanting information and support. EGSSC is developing its existing toy library in collaboration with a voluntary organisation 'Wooden Spoon'. It is building partnerships through the dual registration of pupils with mainstream schools; joint training days with mainstream school staff; and team teaching. It provides 'inreach' for pupils at Key Stages 3 and 4 with Asperger's syndrome. Also, adult students studying for a postgraduate certificate in education and their tutors attend workshops at EGSSC (250 over two days).

The school believes that the main benefit of multi-agency working is the potential for the whole to be greater than the sum of its parts. Working together around a common vision can enable each agency to see and exploit 'synergies' with each partner working towards its desired outcomes while supporting the targets of others. The Every Child Matters outcomes provide a framework for this by seeking to establish congruent but distinctive objectives appropriate to each agency. The targets are frequently not achievable by one agency working in isolation. The 'localisation' agenda placing schools at the heart of integrated and coherent services to the community engages schools with statutory and voluntary agencies in ways not previously possible or expected.

education, social services and health services, with teachers, residential social workers, an art therapist, a psychotherapist and a cognitive behavioural therapist all working together on the same site.

Assessment and the Common Assessment Framework

Assessment associated with preparing a statement of SEN is often a kind of serial assessment in which each professional contributing writes what they know of the pupil and what they recommend in relative isolation, rather like a series of railway carriages.

The Common Assessment Framework (CAF) for children and young people is meant to provide a nationally standardised approach to conducting an assessment of a child's 'needs' and deciding how they should be 'met'. CAF is intended to be holistic and evidence-based and is expected to promote better, earlier identification of children's 'additional needs' and improve multi-agency working. It is scheduled to be implemented from 2006 to 2008.

In a special school, joint assessment may overlap with day-to-day practice where the special school staff work together routinely on shared assessments. Also, joint assessments are often carried out both as an expression of joint day-to-day working and to further support such working by the professionals concerned.

In Rectory Paddock School (www.rectorypaddock.bromley.sch.uk) emphasis is placed on multi-disciplinary working between teachers, nurses, physiotherapists, speech and language therapists, occupational therapists and others. An example of this is multi-disciplinary, child-led, dynamic assessment where a music therapist, physiotherapist and speech and language therapist work together to build up a picture, for example of a child's opportunities to communicate, his means of doing so and his motivation. Activities in the assessment session may range from unstructured tasks to more structured ones and each therapist has pre-planned assessment aims. But there is a continuous dialogue between the therapists to reflect and clarify issues as they arise.

The school has written and videotaped evidence of this approach, which is used to share information with parents, teachers and others.

Liaison

Liaison may involve staff who visit the special school perhaps only for a few hours a week or even less frequently but who are available for advice or consultation or who contribute to case study discussions on a child. Where the special school is the venue for such meetings, several professionals who need to attend meetings may already be based at the school.

Liaison at senior level is assisted when senior representatives of various professional groups have a place in the senior management team. For example, the Senior Management Team (SMT) would include the head teacher, head of education, head of care and head of therapy as well as the bursar. Such arrangements can help ensure that longer term planning takes place that encourages the day-to-day work among different professionals. For example, time can be allocated to joint planning between teachers and therapists for joint assessment and interventions.

Thinking points

Readers may wish to consider with regard to their school:

*   the extent to which national and local top-down developments reflect what is already happening in the special school;
*   how clearly defined joint enterprises can help ensure close multi-professional working for the benefit of pupils and parents.

Key resources

Many special schools support and encourage multi-professional working in advance of approaches recommended in many special education texts and so form a useful source of information. Examples may be found in the case studies in the present volume and in Farrell, M. (2006) *Celebrating the Special School*, London, David Fulton Publishers, *passim*.

Address

DfES Publications centre, tel: 0845 602 2260; e-mail: dfes@prolog.uk.com.

Tunnel

Chapter 8

Strong home–school partnership

As long ago as 1978 the 'Warnock Report' stated: 'the successful education of children with special educational needs is dependent on the full involvement of parents: indeed, unless parents are seen as equal partners in the educational process, the purpose of our report will have been frustrated' (DES, 1978).

This chapter concerns the development of partnership between the family of a child with SEN attending a special school and the school itself. I consider the family in a sense that sees the prime importance of the child's parents but also recognises a broader perspective of family support. The chapter outlines some of the features parents value about special schools.

I touch on parent partnership services and outline the nature of home–school agreements within the context of home–school policy. The chapter examines consultation with parents and the quality of communications. An approach to helping establish sustainable levels of involvement is described. Finally, practical suggestions for developing home–school partnership are discussed. (See, for example, Box 8.1.)

The child's family and the school

Working closely with parents is an aspiration of all schools and a continuing theme in government guidance, for example the *Special Educational Needs Code of Practice* (DfES, 2001a) devotes a chapter to 'Working in Partnership with Parents'. Also, specific guidance on seeking to understand what parents of children with SEN might need is available (e.g. Greenwood, 2002).

In recent decades, ideas and approaches have been developing concerning working with parents of children with SEN (Mittler and Mittler, 1994; Hornby, 1995; Dale, 1996; Carpenter, 1997; Randall and Parker, 1999). In the context of early intervention, the approach of parents supporting other parents has been recognised (Hornby, 1995). (See Box 8.1.)

Cunningham and Davis (1985) identified three models of the relationship between parents and professionals: the 'expert', 'transplant' and 'consumer' models, and it has been suggested the 'consumer' model marked the beginning of a more equal partnership between parents and service providers, with

Box 8.1 BROADFIELD SPECIALIST SCHOOL (SEN/ COGNITION AND LEARNING), LANCASHIRE

Broadfield Specialist School, Accrington, Lancashire is a co-educational school educating 120 pupils aged 4 to 16 years who have moderate or severe learning difficulties with some pupils having attention deficit hyperactivity disorder. The school also has a unit for children with autism.

Although face-to-face contact with parents is constrained by pupils being escorted to school on private transport, the school makes considerable efforts to involve parents. The school has a parents' group, organised by a parent governor, which meets regularly. Parents work in the school, for example hearing pupils read, taking care of the school library and helping with fund-raising and social events.

Parents' views are gathered through an annual questionnaire, the analysed outcomes of which are sent to parents, and individual education plans are sent home for parents' comments and contributions. Parents are invited to contribute to decision-making such as helping write a bid for extended school funding and identifying what they required from an after-school club.

Parents for whom English is an additional language are telephoned weekly by a bilingual assistant and are visited regularly at home.

Courses organised by the parental liaison coordinator are offered to parents and include 'parents as educators' and 'information and communications technology' and several parents have obtained accreditations for these.

Teachers use home–school diaries to aid communication and the speech and language therapist makes home visits to offer support with communication systems. There is a termly newsletter and merit assemblies to which parents are invited. A parents' room is provided with publications offering advice and information. Each term parents are invited to an informal event and a crèche is provided.

the parent exercising control over the selection of services and the working relationship between parents and professionals being characterised by: 'a shared sense of purpose; a willingness to negotiate; sharing of information; shared responsibility; joint decision-making and accountability' (Carpenter, 2001: 278). Two further related models are also pertinent: 'empowerment' and 'negotiating' models. An 'empowerment' model (Appleton and Minchcom, 1991) includes a recognition of the family as a system and of the family's social network, while a 'negotiating' model (Dale, 1996) emphasises collaboration and negotiated joint decision-making.

The family of a child attending special school (like that of any other child) may take different forms. It may be a nuclear or extended family. It may be isolated or may be well supported by a network of people beyond the biological and relational family circle: neighbours, friends, voluntary workers, colleagues from work and others. The siblings of children with SEN may provide important support (Glynne-Rule, 1995) and grandparents may make a valuable contribution (Mirfin-Veitch and Bray, 1997)

In order to form a close partnership with the child's home, it is self-evident that the school needs to know the family circumstances and any changes in them. Any partnership that the school may develop is then more likely to be helpful because it will take into consideration the family's situation. Multi-professional working has the potential at its most organised to contribute to this in that different services of health, social care and education can better share and pool information and insights. (See also Chapter 7 'Confident multi-professional working' in this volume.)

What parents value about special schools

Examples of what parents value about special schools include those recorded in *The Report of the Special Schools Working Group* (DfES, 2003c: 123–51); the opinions of parents in Staffordshire reported by Wilmott (2006); and with regard to individual schools, the views of parents whose children are educated at Rectory Paddock School, Orpington, Kent; New Rush Hall School, Ilford; Freemantles School, Surrey; the Royal School for the Blind, Liverpool; Peterhouse School, Southport; and Brooklands School, Surrey (Farrell, 2006f). Reports of special schools published by OfSTED following their inspections of schools also give indications of the involvement of parents and the extent to which they value the particular special school concerned.

Sources such as those above indicate that parents' views include that they value: that special schools can offer a much less restricted environment for pupils with health or intimate care needs (DfES, 2003c: 128); the availability of 'regular health input into special schools' (ibid.: 142); the high-quality specialist support (ibid.: 133); the safe environment where the child feels safe too, and 'lots of staff support' (Farrell, 2006f: 31); the fact that there is 'more support than in mainstream and you can talk to the staff' (ibid.: 33); that the staff are 'properly trained' and the ethos is very happy (ibid.: 33); and that there is an 'openness and willingness to communicate' (ibid.: 36). (See, for example, Box 8.2.)

One parent observed of a special school:

> I find all the staff very approachable and they are happy to help and offer suggestions for any problems we may be experiencing . . . Daily comments in the diary let me feel part of my child's day which wouldn't happen without the diary as my son is non verbal. I am aware of my son's individual education plan and do what I can at home to support my son meeting his targets.
>
> (Farrell, 2006f: 34)

Box 8.2 ASHLEY SCHOOL, SUFFOLK

Ashley School, Lowestoft, Suffolk is a co-educational day and boarding community school for 125 pupils aged 7 to 16 years having moderate learning difficulties, some of whom have behavioural, emotional and social difficulties. There is an outreach service at Key Stage 1 (5 to 7 years) and Key Stage 4 (14 to 16 years) and a number of work-related learning programmes managed by the school promoting inclusion and shared learning with learners in local high schools. The school offers after-school activities four nights per week and residential options to support children's care needs and their social and emotional development.

Home–school partnership has been enhanced in several ways. A Pupil Services Manager, a qualified social worker, leads the residential care programme, and encourages joint working with social care and health professionals beyond the school and the coordination of welfare issues for all the learners in school. A team of four childcare practitioners and a school support worker support him.

In 2000, with support from the Children's Fund, the school set up information and support services for parents of learners at Ashley School and those educated at local primary schools. The school appointed a part-time project worker, provided initial training and set up the following services: individual parent access to drop-in sessions; signposting to local services for children; individual parent-to-parent support; and parental group sessions.

Learning from the benefits of the project, the school appointed and funded a full-time school support worker, making the role more focused on working with parents and learners 'in need' attending Ashley School that meet several of the section 17 Children Act children in need criteria. The school aims to give each piece of support work a time allocation and specify outcomes, although some families 'in need' require ongoing support. The Pupil Services Manager provides supervision.

A referral system is in place and increased support has been provided to identify learners at all key stages. This includes promoting pupils' access to the school's residential provision; and reducing isolation and aiding transition: into school from mainstream, between Key Stages within school, and into college. The school has supported individual parents to better understand and manage their child's SEN and facilitate parent-to-parent support groups and improve attendance.

The school support worker role has enabled teaching and classroom support staff to focus on teaching and learning and school improvement and has supported the implementation of the workload agreement in the school.

It has also improved communication and networking between the school and other agencies working in the local community. The person appointed is an experienced learning support assistant committed to improving learners' access to the curriculum, their attainment and personal development. She understands the culture and aims of the school, the roles and responsibilities of staff and their working practices; is an active listener and a good communicator and has the capacity to build trust. She can also 'tell it as it is' when needed.

A recent evaluation detailing issues, input and outcomes of work with 47 learners demonstrates the significant added value of this role regarding positive outcomes for parents and learners.

Parent partnerships

Under the Education Act 1996, there is a statutory duty on LEAs to make arrangements for all parents who have a child with SEN to have access to parent partnership services and to make informal arrangements for resolving any disagreements about SEN. Parent partnership services aim to help parents make informed decisions about their child's education, providing information, advice and support for the parents of children with SEN. They also seek to contribute to the five outcomes of Every Child Matters.

The National Parent Partnership Network (NPPN) promotes parent partnership work. As statutory services, local parent partnership services offer information, advice and support for the parents of children and young people with SEN. They can put parents in contact with other local organisations and help ensure parents' views are known and that these inform local policy and practice. For all parents who want it, the parent partnership services will provide access to an Independent Parental Supporter on whom parents can rely to offer independent advice and help to guide them through the system. Most services are based in local authorities or Children's Trusts while some are in the voluntary sector. All provide impartial advice and support to parents.

Home–school policies, home–school agreements and relationship building

Home–school partnership can be focused through a clear home–school policy and through related planning and action, regularly reviewed by the school's governing body. Within this context, home–school agreements can be an effective initial incentive, aiming to improve the links between the school and parents by providing a framework for the development of that partnership. It is not only the agreement that can be a useful underpinning, but the process of discussion and consultation leading to it which can help make clearer the respective roles and expectations of parents, pupils and the school.

The intention is that home–school agreements should lead to better communication so that parents are clearer about their child's progress and what is being taught, and the school is more aware of any aspects of home life that may influence the child's education. It is hoped that in specific areas, the home–school agreement will help teachers and parents work together more effectively, for example with regard to dress codes, bullying or health education.

This fine situation may be particularly so when the documents are first discussed and agreed, but the intentions can fade and the agreements become mere paper exercises. It is important that face-to-face contacts with parents and continued efforts to build and maintain good relationships continue so that parents can also be helped to support their child's home learning better. The annual review process of statements of SEN and other meetings all contribute to this.

Consulting parents

Parents, it is recognised, are the child's first and most enduring educators (QCA, 1999) making the close working of parents and teachers and others vital in ensuring the child gets the best out of education. Also, it has been suggested, 'A happy and open relationship with parents, based on confidence and trust, is crucial to the building of a successful relationship with their children' (Whitbread, 1996). Where pupils have emotional and behavioural difficulties, working with parents has been found to have an effect in helping manage the child (Henggeler, 1999).

Clearly, where parents are regularly and purposely consulted, their views are more securely known and can be more effectively taken into consideration. Among ways of consulting parents are questionnaires, which might be distributed annually or when there is need for gleaning parents' views on a particular matter. Group meetings between teachers and other staff and parents and individual interviews between a member of staff and a parent can provide more detailed information. The school–home association can be a further vehicle for consultation.

I suggest it is helpful if the purpose of the consultation is made clear to parents at the outset. Indeed it may be the former views of parents that have led to the consultation, for example where some parents have expressed a concern about pupils' behaviour at break times and the school agrees to consult more widely to explore the extent to which the concerns are shared and what parents perceive can be done to improve matters.

Where consultation has taken place, the school will need to decide how the outcomes of the consultation are collated and presented to parents and others and what further action might be suggested from the findings. The

---

Box 8.3 APPLETREE SCHOOL, CUMBRIA

Appletree School, Kendal, Cumbria (www.appletreeschool.co.uk) is a residential primary independent special school approved by the Secretary of State
and offering 52-week care. It educates up to 12 boys and girls aged 6 to 12
years who have behavioural, emotional and social difficulties but who are
academically able. A clinical team comprises Appletree staff, and draws also
on staff from the local Primary Care Trust, and the National Society for the
Prevention of Cruelty to Children.

The school works with families and foster families seeking to involve them
in their child's provision. Once placed in Appletree School, children visit home
according to a plan agreed in their programme. While a child is visiting home,
the school offers support as necessary. This is usually through telephone
contact but if required might involve a member of staff visiting the home,
perhaps bringing the child back with them to the school.

Families also visit Appletree where their stay in local hotels is funded by
the school. The school works to ensure that during their stay the parents'
contacts with their child are as positive as possible. This is intended to give
the opportunity for relationships to be rebuilt, leading to the child's successful
later reintegration. A clinical psychologist supports families who require more
specialist help in dealing with the issues that have led to the child's placement
in Appletree.

The school regards its strong partnership with families as a key contributor
to successful return to their family and to their local day school whether this
be special or mainstream. Between 2000 and 2005, Appletree reintegrated
75 per cent of its children to their family or foster family and day schools.

---

clear and fair presentation of findings with opportunities to discuss them can
go some way towards reassuring parents that any concerns are being taken
seriously.

Against such a background of consultation, various aspects of school life
can act to improve the participation of parents. (See, for example, Box 8.3.)

A focus on the quality of communication

As a thread running through much home–school partnership, the quality of
communications can be a useful aspect for a school to review and improve.
Among the questions a special school might wish to consider are:

- how are telephone communications logged and dealt with?
- how does the school respond to letters or notes from parents?
- what impression does the quality of paper and the layout of letters or forms convey about the school?
- is ICT effectively used to personalise certain letters?
- if home visits are made what is their purpose and are they achieving it? and
- what do parents themselves say about the quality of communication with the school and how it can be improved?

In reviewing these matters, the school may find that it can do much to improve communications before consulting parents and others about how it can improve further. For example, in reviewing home visits, it may emerge that staff are not clear about the purpose and expected outcomes and that information from home visits is not effectively shared as appropriate. An examination of the issues and how matters can be improved then putting more effective strategies in place and monitoring them can precede consultation with parents about how the usefulness of the visits can be further improved.

Levels of parental involvement

While the principle of parental involvement is widely accepted and the range of areas in which parents might be involved is wide, it is important that the school has some kind of model for channelling involvement and prioritising what it and parents consider helpful. A blanket notion that all parents should be involved in everything is neither practicable nor desirable. Similarly, schools should be clear about what they could be offering parents and families as first priorities.

A model for collaborating with parents in order to help pupils experiencing difficulties at school is suggested by Hornby (2003: 131), which may have wider application for work with parents of pupils with SEN more generally. It distinguishes between what it is considered parents 'need' and what it can reasonably be expected they can contribute.

Parents' *needs* are considered to be for communication with the school (which all parents need); liaison such as that taking place at parent–teacher meetings (which most parents need); education such as parents' workshops (which many need); and support such as counselling (which some need).

Parents' *contributions* are considered as information, for example about the child's strengths (which all parents can provide); collaboration, for example with behaviour programmes or supporting a pupil's individual education plans (to which most parents could contribute); resources, such as being a classroom aid (which many could contribute); and helping develop policy, for example being a parent governor of the school (which some could contribute).

The model leaves open the exact interpretation of what the expressions 'most', 'many' and 'some' might mean and schools will bring their own judgements to bear on, for example, whether it is reasonable to expect 'many' parents to contribute at a level suggested by being a classroom aid. Nevertheless the basic structure of the model with a graduated view of the parents' proposed needs and their contribution seems to be a helpful one.

Of course, the use of the term 'need' is difficult as it raises questions about who is deciding what the supposed need is and how anyone would know when that need was fulfilled. Where a school appears to be determining what parents 'need', it seems sensible to check that parents see matters in a similar way.

One approach would be to discuss the model with parents and see if agreement can be reached about the model itself and implications for using a differential approach to involvement. If reasonable estimates can be agreed about levels of involvement, the school and families can better plan the time and other resources that are necessary. The success of the approach can be monitored and evaluated. Establishing the views of parents on the issue of participation (perhaps through annual parents' meetings and annual questionnaires) are ways of helping find out whether their level of involvement is at its optimum at any given time. As parents, what they want, and what the school offers change over time, the continuing process of monitoring and evaluation can help maintain high levels of parent satisfaction about the school's partnership with them.

Some practical ways of developing home–school partnership

The school's home–school partnership approaches may include:

- providing information about types of SEN and practical strategies for coping;
- putting parents in touch with support groups locally and nationally;
- making school premises available for various activities such as a parents' support group;
- having displays of literature such as leaflets and lists of Internet sites;
- being a 'one stop' point of contact for other services;
- providing opportunities for family learning;
- offering training, for example in supporting home learning;
- supporting a home–school association; and
- participating in and encouraging interagency support for families.

Carpenter (2001: 281) offers practical suggestions as starting points for schools to evaluate their approaches to working with parents and families. These include: home visits; events for the whole family; shared planning and recording; opportunities for celebration such as awarding achievement certificates; playgroups; parent support groups; home–school diaries in written or audio form or using symbols; telephone contact; a parent's library; and shared training.

As well as more general involvement, particular subjects and areas of the curriculum provide good foci of involvement for parents. Panter (2001: 50) suggests specific examples of involving parents in their child's mathematics learning. These include using home routines and other times when the child and parent are together to encourage mathematics skills. For example, the parent may ask whether a container of liquid is full or empty, half full or a quarter full. They might ask the child what time it is or how long it is to a specified time such as dinnertime.

Parent workshops might help parents better understand how to help their child. Joint parent and pupil workshops can allow parents to see what their child can do or enable the sharing of the language of mathematics. Also, mathematics days in school holidays may allow parents to join pupils for part of the time and the school can create mathematics trails with parents, which they can do with their children (ibid.: 50).

In addition to the support to parents that teachers, teaching assistants and others routinely give, from lending a listening ear to in-depth discussions, other staff can play influential roles in supporting parents. The school social worker through home visits and through enabling contacts with other parents can be a strong source of support. Where the school has a family therapist, or a school social worker, she can form a special link between the world of home and school. Portage workers visiting the home of a preschool child can form strong links with parents.

Kirby and Drew (2003: 76) suggest, among factors that can help in supporting parents: giving enough time for parents to talk and being prepared to listen; providing information that parents can take away and the opportunity to come back and discuss it; and gaining the collaboration of others working with the child and linking the services together for the parent.

Among other innovative ways of involving parents and enabling discussion are weekly lunches hosted by the teacher to which parents are invited (Webster-Stratton, 1999) and inviting small groups of parents to attend informal meetings at the school during school time (Layzell, 1995).

Through the consultation process discussed earlier, the special school may wish to focus on the views of parents at different periods in their child's schooling to the extent that views and requirements differ. For example, the school may wish to collate views relating to transitions such as the arrival of pupils in the nursery or transfer from nursery to primary, primary to secondary, and secondary to further and higher education phases. Such phases have been discussed in relation to the support that families of a child with visual impairment might need (Stone, 1997: 392–3).

More recent initiatives include the encouragement of extended schools focusing on support for parents (DfES, 2002). See also the section in Chapter 1 on 'extended schools and children's centres' pp. 6–8).

Thinking points

Readers may wish to consider in relation to a particular special school:

- what strategies will be developed for and what resources will be directed at consulting parents and families;
- how coherently home–school partnership policy, planning and practice hold together;
- how effective is the system of monitoring and evaluation of parental satisfaction and how well the school responds to issues arising.

Key texts

Greenwood, C. (2002) *Understanding the Needs of Parents: Guidelines for Effective Collaboration with Parents of Children with Special Educational Needs*, London, David Fulton Publishers.

This book may interest staff in both special schools and ordinary schools.

Hornby, G. (2003) 'Counselling and Guidance of Parents' in Hornby, G., Hall, E. and Hall, C. (eds) *Counselling Pupils in Schools: Skills and Strategies for Teachers*, London, Routledge-Falmer, pp. 129–40.

The chapter suggests the differential approach to parents' involvement. While it concerns a model for collaborating with parents in order to help pupils experiencing difficulties at school, it may have application for work with parents of pupils with SEN.

Boathouse

Chapter 9

Dynamic pupil participation

While pupils' participation in their education and in school life, like a school's partnership with parents, is generally accepted as self-evidently positive, the detail of how such participation might be encouraged and sustained is something to which good special schools expend considerable thought and effort.

This chapter examines what pupils appear to value in general about special schools. I look at pupil participation and consultation. The chapter considers approaches to, and vehicles for, participation first in general terms and then with regard to consulting pupils and using data gathered as a result of consultation. I examine some elements of participation: personalised learning and learning to learn; making choices and decisions; pupils participating in planning and evaluating learning; and pupil discussions and decisions about their future. Finally, a project involving a group of local education authority special schools is outlined.

What pupils value in general about special schools

Features that pupils value about special schools were indicated in discussion groups held in connection with the preparation of *The Report of the Special Schools Working Group* (DfES, 2003c). Pupils who had moved from an ordinary school to a day or residential special school found their special schools 'friendlier' and 'nicer' and said the special school 'doesn't make a fuss about my medication' and that they had 'more friends – I can walk to school with them' (ibid.: 157). Some felt that ordinary schools did not have the skills to really listen to and respect them, for example, 'not understanding special communication needs, not allowing sufficient time, not looking at the best way of offering accessible information' (ibid.: 167).

The book *Celebrating the Special School* included information from a survey conducted by the pupils of Walton Hall School, Staffordshire; the comments of pupils at New Rush Hall School, Ilford; and the views of ex-pupils of Coxlease School, Hampshire and the Mulberry Bush School, Oxfordshire. These suggested pupils enjoyed the effects of the special school having high

Box 9.1 STANLEY SCHOOL, WIRRAL

Stanley School, Wirral (www.stanleyschool.org.uk), is a local authority community day special school educating 90 pupils aged 2 to 11 years with severe learning difficulties, some of whom have autistic spectrum disorder. The school gained an achievement award in 2002; it is accredited by the National Autistic Society; its Early Learning department was accredited by the Effective Early Learning Project and is an Investor in Children.

Pupil participation is encouraged in several ways. For example, participation in learning through links with a mainstream primary school is monitored. The site is shared with the local primary school and some Stanley pupils join pupils from the primary school for some teaching, lunch sessions and leisure pursuits, all of which are planned, have clear objectives, are recorded and are agreed in consultation with parents. This helps ensure that participation in different groups is enjoyable and leads to better progress. The progress is monitored through a matrix devised by the school. Pupils are assessed on a five-point scale which tracks increasing levels of participation as shown by the amount of time they spend in mainstream school, the type of activity in which they participate, the level of supervision required and the nature of the targets set for them. The school has clear evidence of progress in these areas and the first pupil to move through this process will start at Stanley's partner school in 2006.

All staff contribute to fuller pupil participation, including teachers, two part-time speech and language therapists, a specialist language support assistant, a visiting occupational therapist, and a physiotherapist. For pupils with very limited communication, the school recognises the need for staff who are well trained, know the pupils well, and work with them long enough to form a close relationship. This allows them to 'read' important signs and act as an advocate on the pupils' behalf.

The curriculum is intended to optimise participation and as well as the National Curriculum framework, includes play, communication and personal independence. For many pupils, additional therapeutic and sensory experiences are part of the curriculum. For some pupils, participation is encouraged through social stories and the social use of language approach (Rinaldi, 1992/2001) and communication passports may be used.

Among strategies aimed at improving the participation of pupils with autistic spectrum disorder are the Teaching and Education of Autistic Children and Communication Handicap (TEACCH) approach. Also the SPELL (Structure, Positive, Empathy, Low arousal Links) framework is used recognising the importance of structure, for example to aid personal autonomy and independence; positive approaches and expectations; empathy; low arousal through a calm and ordered approach and environment; and links, for example between the components of the pupil's life or therapeutic programme to encourage consistency. (See also www.nas.org.uk.) Aids to communication such as electronic talkers are used as necessary.

Integration matrix

Supervision	Activity	Time	Targets
Level 1 Group activity with close supervision at Stanley (KS1 and 2) or playgroup (EY)	Low demand social activities, e.g. soft play, outdoor play, cubs, choral assembly, playgroup	Short duration – 20–30 minutes with class or group	General aims for group activities
Level 2 Close supervision – additional support from LSA within small group	General class activities – Reception/Year 1 pupils working within appropriate Key Stage	30–45 minutes	General objectives identified on statement, e.g. play and social interaction skills
Level 3 LSA provides additional support for whole class	Subject-based activity, e.g. PE, ICT, music with appropriate year group	60 minutes	Targets relating to the generalisation of skills across different settings identified on IEP, e.g. language and communication, play
Level 4 Pupil working independently/with limited support – small group and class activities	Subject-based activity, e.g. literacy, numeracy with appropriate year group	10% + timetable	Specific targets on IEP relating to cognitive achievement which can be addressed during integrated sessions
Exit criteria			
Level 5 Pupil working independently within appropriate year group	Wide range of NC subjects – pupil working individually, in small groups and with the whole class	50% timetable	Pupil able to achieve specific targets with limited level of support available

aspirations for pupils, the enriched social experiences, better preparation for adult life and other benefits (Farrell, 2006f: 41–4).

Given that it is accepted that special schools continue to listen to pupils and engage with them, pupil participation is a perspective facilitating this.

Pupil participation and consultation

If participation is regarded as 'the process of sharing in decisions which affect one's life and the life of the community in which one lives' it may be argued that the 'understanding, competence and commitment to democratic participation can only be achieved through practice and experience' (Lansdown, 1995: 17). In other words, school pupils may learn something about participation from the content of the school curriculum but can also learn a great deal from participating fully in school life and in their learning.

Within the context of pupil participation, pupil consultation has been said to rest on the principle that 'pupils can bring something worthwhile to discussions about schooling' (Flutter and Rudduck, 2004: 5). Where consultation includes discussion of the way pupils learn and how effectively they are taught, there are indications that this can improve performance (Watkins, 2001: *passim*). Also, teacher–pupil dialogue around metacognition to 'develop a shared perspective of the learning process' is considered to contribute to a sense of 'competency and self worth' (Doran and Cameron, 1995: 22).

A 'ladder' of pupil participation has been proposed (Flutter and Rudduck 2004: 16; from Hart, 1997). This ascends from the lowest rung of 'pupils not consulted'; through 'listening to pupils'; 'pupils as active participants'; and 'pupils as researchers' up to the highest rung where pupils are 'fully active participants and co-researchers'.

In special schools, consulting pupils about their learning appeared to be associated with improved confidence and self-esteem, better engagement and motivation to learn, and more active membership of the school community (Jelly et al., 2000).

Approaches to pupil participation can embrace links with mainstream schools and other features as the example of Stanley School, Wirral (see Box 9.1 on p. 113), and the matrix and the block graph in Figure 9.1 (p. 116) indicate. The graph is one of a number used by the school and the school also monitors individual pupils using the matrix.

Approaches to and vehicles for participation

General points

Approaches to participation in schools have been differentiated according to the extent of the initiative (e.g. whole school or a specified group of pupils);

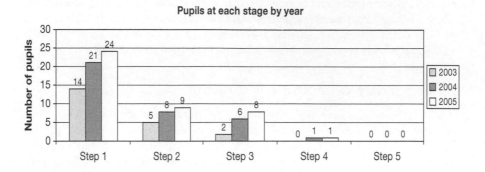

Figure 9.1 Stanley Matrix – steps

the scope (broad or narrow); the timescale; and the degree of integration into the school's system (e.g. a whole school process or one teacher's practice) (Flutter and Rudduck, 2004: 23–4).

Related to this, various approaches have been characterised where schools have used consultation: as a 'wide angle' approach seeking to identify generalised problems; as a way of focusing on particular issues or groups of pupils; as part of the school's systems of monitoring and evaluating; as a way of supporting individual pupils having difficulties with their learning; as part of continuing school self-review; and as a way of developing a more democratic school system (Flutter and Rudduck, 2004: 25).

Consulting pupils

The school may consult pupils in various ways including questionnaires, dialogue, a school council, advocacy and particular aids to communication.

Questionnaires may be used that allow pupils to express views anonymously if they wish. These need to be carefully designed and it may be useful to try out the draft on a few pupils to ensure that the questions are unambiguous and relevant. An example of a questionnaire used by pupils evaluating lessons is provided in Sweyne Park School, a mainstream comprehensive school in Essex, which gives an idea of what might be developed (Fuller and Rudduck, 2004: 54).

Dialogue can probe the views of pupils. Strategies for ascertaining pupils' views can take into account particular types of SEN. For example, Lewis (2004) lists some aspects of methods relevant to chronologically young children or 'developmentally young' children. These include:

- permit or encourage 'don't know' responses and requests for clarification;
- stress not knowing the events or views of the child to counter the child's assumption that the adult knows the answer (the child tends to be more suggestible if the adult has credibility and rapport with the child);
- use statements rather than questions to trigger fuller responses from children;
- if using questions, use an appropriate level of generality (for example 'open or moderately focused questions seem to generate more accurate responses from children with learning difficulties than do highly specific questions');
- limit 'yes/no' questions to avoid acquiescence, particularly for pupils with learning difficulties; and
- aim for an uninterrupted narrative.

(from Lewis, 2004: 4–6)

Also, materials used when seeking to explore the views of children with learning difficulties include such sources as: the guidelines *Listening to Children with Communication Support Needs* (Aitken and Millar, 2002); *How It Is* (Marchant and Cross, 2002); and projects such as *Can You Hear Us? Including the Views of Disabled Children and Young People* (Whittles, 1998).

In terms of being a form of consultation, the school council with class or year group representatives may be adept at reflecting the views of other pupils and representing them. In the sense of participation, the school council may discuss matters such as school rules; improving the quality of break times, food at lunchtimes and similar matters of importance to pupils. But they may also look into and discuss matters that concern curriculum development and teaching and learning. As suggested by Mittler (2001: 341) they may discuss the policy of visitors entering the classroom and access to their work and files.

Advocacy support may help pupils express feelings and views and can facilitate self-advocacy. A key underpinning is the encouragement of effective communication. For all pupils, opportunities to develop better communication are important. Approaches can vary in relation to the type of SEN, although the examples given below are not intended to suggest that the approaches are necessarily exclusive to particular types of SEN. They include for deaf children oral/aural approaches, total communication and sign bilingualism (Farrell, 2006e: 36–7). For children who are deafblind approaches include intensive interaction, co-creative communication, resonance work, co-active movement and signing, burst-pause activities, routines and scripts, and hand-over-hand work (Farrell, 2006e: 51–2).

Pupils may use a camera to take pictures of aspects of school or home that help them in their learning and later discuss these with the teacher and other pupils. Pupils might freely write about their views or keep a learning log about aspects of lessons they find useful or unhelpful.

For pupils with severe learning difficulties, augmentative and alternative communication and intensive interaction may be used and communication may be encouraged through music (Farrell, 2006b: 44–6). With regard to learners who have behavioural, emotional and social difficulties, various strategies may be aimed at encouraging the communication of feelings, such as aspects of emotional literacy (Farrell, 2006a: 32–3), counselling (ibid.: 57–9) and aspects of the curriculum that can enhance communication including drama, play and music (ibid.: 60). For pupils with communication difficulties interventions may apply to difficulties with speech, grammar, meaning, the use of language and comprehension (Farrell, 2006d: *passim*). With reference to autism, various interventions aim to enhance communication including signing systems for communication, the Picture Exchange Communication System and musical interaction therapy (ibid.: 80–2). (See, for example, Box 9.2.)

Using the data from consultation

In using the data gathered as a result of consultation, the special school may wish to pose itself several questions.

Before data is gathered, how will the school make the purpose of the consultation clear and explain to teachers, pupils and others how it is proposed to use the data? Once the data is gathered, how exactly will it be analysed? Will it be examined to explore issues emerging (if the approach has been 'wide angle') or is it intended to throw light on the particular issues of enquiry (where the focus has been more specific)? Will the data be analysed in terms of groups within the school – boys and girls, pupils of different ages and so on – where this assists the enquiry? How will the information once it is collated be conveyed? Verbally? Using charts or diagrams? As a written report? A combination of these? To whom will the information be presented? Teachers, pupils, parents?

Some elements of participation

Participation may be expressed in various features of school life, many of them interrelated.

Personalised learning and learning to learn

Personalised learning, an approach to learning and teaching, involves shaping education to what are perceived as the individual learner's 'needs', interests and aptitudes and the way the pupil learns (www.standards.dfes.gov.uk/personalisedlearning). It is envisaged in five components: assessment for learning with particular reference to summative aspects (e.g. Black *et al.*, 2002: 7); effective teaching and learning strategies (including information

Box 9.2 ROSEWOOD SCHOOL, SOUTHAMPTON

Rosewood School, Southampton is a non-maintained special school for up to 40 children with profound and multiple learning difficulties. Run by the Rose Road Association, a local charity, the school offers a specialised curriculum focusing on the individual needs of each pupil, developing key skills in communication, cognitive development, environmental control technology, physical skills, and personal, social and health education. The National Curriculum is used to provide a breadth of experience and learning opportunities in which to teach the key skills. The school has an attached therapy suite enabling staff to meet the therapeutic and medical needs of the pupils. The therapy team consists of physiotherapists, occupational therapist, a full-time nurse and two healthcare support workers, a hydrotherapy support worker, a speech and language therapist and a music therapist.

The school regards the development of a child's communication as central to its work and as a prerequisite for achieving success across the curriculum and has focused on assessment, curriculum planning and passport design. The school begins with a thorough assessment of the child's communicative abilities. Teaching staff, working in close partnership with the speech and language therapist, devised the 'Rosewood School Communication Assessment', identifying six strands of communication: Interaction; the use of hands; tactile communication; vision; vocalisation; and hearing. Three developmental stages were agreed, pre-intentional (P scale reference 1–2), intentional (P scale 2–3) and formal (P scale 3–4). The assessment provides an overview of how the child currently communicates and his areas of strength.

So that the assessment could be used to inform future planning, the school devised a curriculum, which further broke down the progress in each stage of development for each identified strand of communication. The school then examined how the assessment information could be most effectively shared through the school, with the child's family and with the wider community. Hence the communication passport was designed (see example p. 121).

The content of the passport was agreed and the sections designed to reflect the school's conviction that the strategies currently used by the child are key. The intention is that by working to consolidate and apply these strategies consistently, the child will be better prepared to succeed in the next steps and in developing higher order skills. Rosewood seeks to resist pressures to push for more formal communication methods before the child is ready and is cautious of advancing technology above the child's communicative capability.

The process of assessment, curriculum planning and passport design is enhanced by the involvement of parents. The user-friendly design and non-technical language in the assessment enables parents to equally contribute with staff on building an accurate profile of the child. The passport has been used by parents to break down barriers in the community and enables members of the general public to be sufficiently confident to engage with the individual child at a level rewarding for both communication partners.

communication technology strategies); curriculum entitlement and choice; school organisation; and strong partnership beyond the school.

For example, a special school might wish to look in more detail at the implications of pupils learning how to learn. This could involve making how the individual pupil learns more explicit to him to help him understand the learning process better. Does he learn well from discussing topics? What preferences does he have regarding the proportion of learning individually and in a group? What aids his memory? From this emerges a picture of how the pupil tends to learn best. The teachers and the pupil can adapt this information to enable increasingly autonomous learning. Elements of this approach have been used in some special schools for decades, for example in metacognition aspects of the Rectory Paddock school (www.rectorypaddock.bromley.sch.uk) curriculum published in the 1980s.

Making choices and decisions

A pupil's choices and decisions indicate participation, making teaching and support that leads to a pupil being able to make choices important. For example, a pupil with profound or severe learning difficulties is likely to require initial help to recognise that there are options and how a choice is signalled. Giving limited choices of two alternatives (e.g. foods) and investing the pupil's perhaps fleeting response with meaning as if a choice had been indicated is one strategy that can over time lead to purposeful choice-making. For some pupils, choices may be more complex, perhaps involving choosing whether to spend more or less time on a topic or whether to pursue something in more depth.

A range of opportunities for choice and decision-making can be offered and include: choices within lessons such as a choice of partner, activity or adult; opportunities to express an opinion; encouragement to discuss feelings and preferences; making decisions about the classroom and activities. This may require explaining choices to pupils and helping them develop skills to make choices and decisions (Gunton, 1990). (See, for example, Box 9.3.)

Box 9.3 COMMUNICATION PASSPORT

Hello my name is _____.
Thank you for looking at my Passport.
It will help both of us if you read it

HOW I COMMUNICATE: I am a modern, happy young lady who is interested in people.
I like people to sit beside me and talk or just sit quietly. I communicate with my emotions: happy and content you will get good eye contact and lots of smiles; sad I will become agitated and do a lot of hand wringing, and I may scream. I choose what I want. I will look intently at my choice and then look intently at you.

I am working on taking turns, one to one with an adult, and using my hands to play with a variety of noisy, bright objects.
If I am sitting quietly please approach me slowly, sit next to me and wait for me to turn to you before you speak.

TALK TO ME ABOUT:
About anything and everything. I especially like to look out of the window or go for a walk in the garden. I like whoever is with me to keep up a running commentary on everything that is going on. I enjoy a hand or foot massage, especially when I am sad or in pain.

MY NEEDS:

IF I ... ...
Am unhappy – I will cry quietly and wring my hands.
Am in pain – I will scream, become very agitated and not lie still. I will put my hands to my mouth and I may bite them.
Want you to go – At home when I want my own time and space I will grumble and wave my arms to show I want to be on my own. I have not really shown this at school.
Want some attention – I will look intently at you and call out.
Am hungry – when offered food I will stop eating when I am no longer hungry. If I reject the food immediately it means I do not like what you have offered me.
Am thirsty – I will look intently at my cup and then at you.

Pupils participating in planning and evaluating learning

Pupils might consider the range of ways in which they learn and what works best or which aspects of a new strategy seem to be effective and which do not. The preferred approach of pupils might include: teacher explanations, visiting speakers, working in pairs and small groups, role play, video recordings, audio material, artefacts, visits to places of interest, and using aspects of information and communication technology.

The pupil and the teacher can work together to implement and evaluate approaches intended to improve the attainment and achievement of the pupil both being responsible in varying degrees for the outcome. Related to this, the forms of assessment that are proposed might be discussed with the pupil.

As a precursor to the Individual Education Plan (IEP) target-setting process, pupils can be consulted about the range of ways in which targets can be reached, that is, learning strategies and forms of support that can facilitate progress. Where pupils are able to be productively involved in the assessment of their learning, this can form a sound basis from which to develop with the pupil strategies aimed at helping progress, often specified in IEPs. A project in which 30 pupils aged 12 to 19 years were supported to set their own learning targets was carried out in Watling View School, Hertfordshire, a special school for pupils with severe or profound and multiple learning difficulties and autistic spectrum disorder (Rose *et al.*, 1996).

Individual pupils can use this information to decide which strategies might be particularly helpful in relation to particular targets. Once the targets and strategies are agreed, ongoing discussions can refer to the strategies and how effective they are turning out to be. Working with the pupil to evaluate progress leads to the setting of new targets and strategies. Discussion with the pupil will reveal whether he understands what the target is and what he has to do to reach it.

The *Special Educational Needs Code of Practice* (DfES, 2001a, especially ch. 3) encourages pupil participation and seeks to involve pupils with SEN in the development and evaluations of their IEPs and behaviour support plans where possible. A balance is sought between encouraging participation and overburdening the pupil when he may not have sufficient experience and knowledge to make judgements without support.

Pupil discussions and decisions about their future

Within a special school where pupil participation is encouraged, discussions about a pupil's future will develop from other broader forms of consultation and participation. There may be general consultation about transition exploring what pupils feel about a change from a primary school to a secondary school or department or what they feel about leaving school and going on to college or training. From this might emerge strategies pupils find helpful such as opportunities to visit new places, talking to pupils who have already made the transition and so on. More formally, much consultation will centre on the pupil's preparation for the annual review meetings in connection with the pupil's statement of SEN and in particular, transition reviews where future work and study options are considered. (See Box 9.4.)

A project involving special schools

Jelly *et al.* (2000) describe a project encouraging pupil participation in seven Essex special schools: Cedar Hall; The Edith Borthwick School; The Hayward School; The Heath School; Longview Unit; Market Field; and Priory School. Three schools described their pupils as having moderate learning difficulties; two as having behavioural, emotional and social difficulties; one as having pupils with moderate to severe learning difficulties; and one was a psychiatric unit. The range of 'focus points' for the project included: pupil involvement in individual education plans and annual review processes; developing thinking skills programmes and materials; a focus on raising self-esteem; and using circle time (Mosley, 1996) to help pupils solve problems (Jelly *et al.*, 2000: 9, paraphrased). Three themes emerging were: pupils' empowerment and enhanced self-esteem; impact on school ethos and culture; and promoting inclusion (ibid.: 11).

An 'audit checklist' summarised the areas of involving pupils in practice:

- Do staff and pupils engage in dialogue about teaching and learning?
- Do staff actively promote pupils' capacity to think?
- Do pupils put forward their own ideas?
- Do staff attend to pupils' views and perspectives?
- Do governors attend to pupils' views and perspectives?
- Do senior managers attend to pupils' views and perspectives? and
- Do school systems and procedures take account of pupils' views and perspectives?

(ibid.: 111–13)

For example, staff engaging pupils in a dialogue about teaching and learning includes staff making use of informal opportunities to have dialogue with pupils; negotiating targets for learning; involving pupils in the annual review process; the use of communication including augmentative and alternative modes to expand pupils' participation; and staff receiving training in such skills as counselling and mentoring (ibid.: 111, paraphrased). Staff promoting pupils' capacity to think includes pupil support through circle of friends, peer tutoring and pupil-to-pupil mentoring relationships (ibid.: 111, paraphrased). (See, for example, Box 9.4.)

Thinking points

Readers may wish to consider with reference to a particular special school:

- how it can further encourage the participation of pupils in school life;
- how it can further encourage individual pupils to participate more fully in their education and monitor their progress.

Key texts

Flutter, J. and Rudduck, J. (2004) *Consulting Pupils: What's in it for Schools?*, London, Routledge-Falmer.

This book reports material from various sources including the Economic and Social Research Council/Teaching and Learning Research Programme Network Project, which explored various aspects of pupil participation in mainstream schools. Appendices include brief guidelines on interviewing pupils and on using questionnaires.

Box 9.4 PUPIL PARTICIPATION

Complete the following with reference to your own school. You may wish to consult pupils.

1   The types of consultation (e.g. wide angle/focused issues) the school uses are _____

2   The school establishes the views of pupils by _____

3   The school responds to the views of pupils by _____

4   Pupils make choices and decisions because the school _____

5   Pupils participate in the identification and assessment of their learning requirements by _____

6   The school involves pupils in the approaches used to improve progress by _____

7   Pupils participate in developing IEP targets and strategies by _____

8   Pupils participate in decisions about their future by _____

Spanish week 1

Chapter 10

Secure funding

This chapter briefly reminds readers of the main differences in the funding of independent, non-maintained and maintained special schools in England. I then look at examples of Department for Education and Skills capital funding: devolved formula capital, modernisation funding and funding under the Building Schools for the Future programme. The chapter examines an example of a government initiative that includes special schools: the specialist special school programme.

I consider the funding of special schools by local authorities both in its usual form and in relation to special schools funded as part of clusters or federations of schools. The importance of the stability of maintained special school funding is emphasised drawing on recent government guidance. I give examples of LAs providing funding to improve special school buildings and facilities. The chapter then considers funding and dual placements between special and mainstream schools and funding arrangements for outreach and other services. I look at strategies to contain the cost to LAs of non-maintained and independent school fees. The chapter examines how a special school might form a charitable organisation to assist fund-raising. Finally, I point out the importance of close liaison between the head teacher, the governors and the bursar.

The funding of different types of special schools

The basic differences in the funding of independent, non-maintained and maintained special schools in England are as follows.

Independent special schools are funded by pupils' fees and may be operated for profit, and an independent school having 25 per cent of its pupils with statements is treated as a special school. Independent special schools may be approved by the Secretary of State under the Education Act 1996 as suitable for the admission of children with statements of SEN. If a special school is not approved, the Secretary of State has to consent before an LA can place a pupil with a statement of SEN in the school. Regulations concerning the approval of independent schools set out the conditions that must be met for initial and continuing approval, covering matters such as the fitness of the

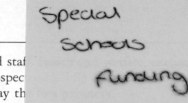

proprietors and staf̲͟   religious education and
the school prospec   ils and meet the costs,
parents may pay th

Non-maintained   subject to regulations
concerning conditi̲   ̲oval by the Secretary of
State relating to m̲   ises, welfare and health
and safety. NMSS,   operated by a charitable
trust and approved as special schools by the Education Act 1996, are funded
mainly by fees charged to LAs placing children there.

Turning to maintained special schools, a community special school is a
state school wholly owned and maintained by the LA. A foundation special
school, being a state school whose governing body is the employer and admissions authority, has more freedom than a community special school to manage
itself and decide on its admissions. The governing body (or a charitable
foundation) owns its land and buildings but funding comes from the LA,
which also pays for any building work.

Capital funding from the Department for Education and Skills

Capital funding can fulfil various purposes. It can be used to build new school
premises, to rebuild a school, for building repairs and maintenance, for
extensions and for modernisation. Most capital funding is allocated to schools
and LAs according to a needs-related formula so LAs can determine their
priorities in line with local asset management planning processes.

Devolved formula capital allocates capital grants directly to schools via
their LAs in line with a formula. This funding is for spending on capital
building needs in accordance with priorities laid out in the LA's asset
management planning process. 'Modernisation' funding is allocated directly
to LAs according to a formula to be invested in line with LAs' asset management plans. The funding under the Building Schools for the Future programme emerged from the Private Finance Initiative (see The Building
Schools for the Future programme below) (www.teachernet.gov.uk/pfi). LAs
normally make bids for additional funding under the 'targeted capital fund'.

Devolved formula capital

Devolved formula capital is allocated to LAs but they must allocate it to
schools using a formula. It therefore gives maintained schools direct funding
to help support the capital needs of their buildings.

Modernisation

Modernisation funding is intended to help raise standards by contributing
to the capital investment needed for school buildings in line with the locally

agreed priorities in the LA asset management plan. It is allocated according to a formula that takes into account building needs as well as pupil numbers.

The Building Schools for the Future programme

The Private Finance Initiative (PFI) involved bringing the private sector more into the provision of assets needed by the public sector, aiming to draw on private sector management and commercial skills. Schools PFI projects included the LA buying asset-based services from the private sector in terms of school buildings; school and classroom facilities (e.g. a sports hall) and services (e.g. information and communication technology services). Usually the PFI contractor owned the assets and was able to make money from their commercial use outside school time. The LA invited the private sector to bid for the PFI contract and entered into a formal commercial contract with the successful bidder. Some of the problems encountered in such arrangements are indicated in the document *Schools PFI – Post-Signature Review by Partnerships UK for the Department for Education and Skills* (Phase 2 Report, May 2005) (DfES/Partnership UK, 2005).

From 2005–6 the PFI became part of the Building Schools for the Future process but the latter can be traced back to 2003. In that year the government announced a capital investment programme for secondary education; formally launching 'Building Schools for the Future' a year later. The programme aims to invest in the rebuilding and renewal of secondary schools to 2016 or 2021. One aspect is the opportunity to bring special schools and mainstream schools closer together physically including collocation (see Chapter 1) (www.teachernet.gov.uk/management/resourcesfinanceandbuilding/schoolbuil dings/sbschoolsforthefuture).

'Partnership for Schools' (PfS) was formed in 2004 to deliver the Building Schools for the Future programme. Owned by the Department for Education and Skills, PfS is managed under a joint venture arrangement between the DfES and Partnership UK.

Government funding and initiatives including special schools: specialist special school status

Funding is linked to certain government initiatives to encourage special schools and others in particular directions. An aspect of some of these schemes is requiring the school to match possible central funding with commitments to similar amounts of funding from community sources such as local businesses. An example is specialist special school status.

A 'specialist schools programme' was extended from its original curriculum-related remit to involve an SEN specialism. Schools specialise in one of the four areas of SEN covered by the *Special Educational Needs Code of Practice* (DfES, 2001a): cognition; behavioural, emotional and social difficulties;

communication; or physical sensory. They are expected to 'share expertise and resources with partner schools, support services, multi-disciplinary agencies and the wider community' (Beatie, 2006: 1, point 1).

They receive £100,000 one-off capital funding, which has to be supplemented by funds raised by the school through sponsorship, and £60,000 for each of the subsequent four years of the programme, which might be used, for example, to fund extra teaching assistants to work in the specialist area or to provide extra staff to work on outreach.

The funding of special schools by LAs

Under section 48 of the School Standards Framework Act 1998, all local authorities are required to establish and maintain a scheme for financing schools. This sets out the relationship between the local authority and the schools it maintains. Regulations list the issues that schemes should address and the Department for Education and Skills provides guidance to local authorities on the more detailed content of their schemes. This guidance is revised from time to time to reflect the changes and amendments to legislation and policy. In addition to this document, local authorities may provide schools with detailed written guidance and advice. Any externally produced material cannot be regarded as adopted procedure and schools must not deviate from local and national statute. An example of local documents may be seen at www.newcastle.gov.uk.

The funding of special schools by LAs may involve the use of a formula for allocating funds according to agreed criteria. Where this includes pupil numbers there may be an agreement that numbers are slightly above the actual number of pupils on roll to allow for new pupils being admitted at different points of the year. Another aspect of the formula may involve an assessment of the level of funding considered suitable for different types of SEN, such as an agreed band of funding for each of: profound and multiple learning difficulty, severe learning difficulty, moderate learning difficulty, and so on. The example of Northumberland LA in Box 10.1 on p. 130 illustrates such an approach.

Special schools funded as part of clusters or federations of schools

As pointed out in Chapter 1, the term 'federations' may refer to partnerships, clusters and collaborative groupings of schools and mergers creating new schools. One aim of federations is to enable schools to build capacity jointly and coherently. A continuum of arrangements is suggested: a 'hard governance federation'; a 'soft governance federation'; a 'soft federation'; and an 'informal, loose federation'. (www.standards.dfes.gov.uk/federations/pdf/Federations Continuum).

Box 10.1 NORTHUMBERLAND LA FUNDING FOR SPECIAL SCHOOLS

Most of the pupil-related funding for special schools and special units in Northumberland LA is place-led, which means that a defined number of places are funded rather than an absolute number of pupils. This allows for the greater fluidity of admissions into specialist provision during the course of a school year relative to the pattern of admissions into mainstream schools.

A matrix is also used to determine an amount of additional, enhanced pupil-related funding that a special school or unit might receive in recognition of the levels of significant additional difficulties that their pupil populations might include each year. A third factor within a special school budget is related to the actual number of pupils on roll in January, while a social deprivation factor is also recognised through the level of free school meals eligibility within the school.

To give an idea of the relative contribution of these elements, a school for pupils with moderate learning difficulties with 115 places received in broad terms £650,000 through place funding, £85,000 through matrix enhancement funding, £25,000 through actual pupil numbers and £10,000 through free school meal eligibility (at 2006 prices). Premises-related funding is of course more site-specific and separate to this.

Each pupil within the special school is compared with a set of descriptors within the matrix that progressively identify an increasing severity of additional difficulty. The matrix determination is not intended to produce an exact correspondence between the actual cost of supporting the individual and the funding required to meet this. Rather, it acknowledges the overall extent of additional difficulty presented by pupils within the school. The special school determines how it makes the best, flexible use of the overall resources available through the LA's formula funding.

The matrix comprises a horizontal aspect that recognises five levels of 'general curriculum modification' ranging in severity from 'generalised moderate difficulties' to 'profound and multiple difficulties', and a vertical aspect that recognises five levels of more specific curriculum modification for: visual impairment; hearing impairment; physical disability; communication difficulty; and behavioural, emotional and social difficulties. A given cell within the matrix generates a number of enhancements that reflect an individual pupil's additional difficulties, if any. These enhancements are then totalled and matched against a fixed value for one enhancement to provide an aggregate funding level that reflects the pupil profile for the whole school.

Among federations including special schools are the Dorset-Chesil Education Partnership comprising mainstream primary and secondary schools and two special schools: Westfield Technology College and Wyvern School. 'The North Somerset 7' federation comprises a group of schools including Ravenswood School, a special school. The West Sussex two-school federation involves a high school and two special schools, St Anthony's and Littlegreen. The East Sussex Partnership of Specialist Schools includes the special school Cuckmere House. West Wiltshire federation includes Springfields, a special school. The Weston Education Partnership comprises four mainstream schools, a college of further education, a pupil referral unit and two special schools: Baytree (see Box 10.2 on p. 132) and West Haven.

The stability of maintained special school funding

The document *The Distribution of Resources to Support Inclusion* (DfES, 2001c) aimed to provide information and suggested approaches for local education authorities to manage SEN expenditure. It concerned both mainstream and special schools, and mentioned various developments such as special schools developing outreach services, which it was considered required 'a review of traditional arrangements for the funding of special schools so that it is possible to support inclusion' (ibid.: section 5, para. 3).

The document notes:

> Special schools are usually funded for the number of places that they provide with the individual place cost determined by the complexity of learning needs that the school has to address. Differential funding may also be available on the basis of age. Place funding has developed to ensure that staffing and other aspects of provision can be as stable as possible within the relatively high cost but small organisations that special schools are. The only exception has tended to be for those who are 'dual registered'.
>
> (ibid.: 5.3)

Alternative approaches were suggested (ibid.: 5.4) for example LAs requiring special schools to support the costs of mainstream placements until a pupil is dual registered or on the roll of a mainstream school (when usual mainstream funding arrangements would come into force).

Regarding maintained special schools, *The Management of SEN Expenditure* (DfES, 2004d) (www.teachernet.gov.uk/senexpenditure) noted: 'Special schools need budgets that are relatively stable but flexible enough to respond to changes in pupils' needs. Many special schools are well placed to develop integrated services to address social and health care needs and outreach' (ibid.: 3).

It was recommended that local authorities 'develop a system of planned funded places in partnership with schools'; 'set out arrangements to support

Box 10.2 BAY TREE SCHOOL, SOMERSET

Bay Tree School, Weston Super Mare, Somerset is a co-educational community school for up to 67 pupils aged 3 to 19 years having autistic spectrum disorder and severe or profound and multiple learning difficulties. In 2002, a local secondary school approached the head teacher, along with another local special school, about the possibility of working with four local secondary schools towards creating a federation of schools.

The secondary school, with the support of the LEA, had made a successful bid to the Department for Education and Skills Innovation Unit and the inclusion of special schools was felt to be an asset. Bay Tree governors enthusiastically agreed and consultants were appointed to help develop an action plan to bid for further funding to develop a federation. The bid was subsequently successful although the amount was considerably less than requested. After initial disappointment about this, Bay Tree adapted its plans and working together continued. After three years of working together Bay Tree recognises the benefits have been considerably broader than the anticipated financial gain. These benefits were expected to be sustainable after funding ended in 2006.

There has been extensive partnership working: between special schools; between special and mainstream schools and the LEA; and between all members of staff and governors. This has involved students working together. It has encouraged team-working skills, and planning and organisational skills and has generated inter-school contracts and services. Training and support has included: joint in-service training; joint continuing professional development opportunities; sharing good practice (e.g. teaching and learning, leadership skills/styles, managing change, management 'tips and wrinkles', differentiation, management of challenging behaviours, subject strengths, accreditation) and special school experiences for initial teacher training students and newly qualified teachers as well as existing staff in secondary schools.

The development of professional relationships has led to students working together on social enterprise schemes. All Bay Tree senior students have regular sessions with mainstream students based in both school settings. One of these was filmed as part of a Qualifications and Curriculum Authority project on P scale guidance and which raised self-esteem for staff and students. Inclusion in the student parliament scheme has given the students from the special school for pupils with severe learning difficulties a broader experience and a wider voice. They have attended sessions and visited the Westminster parliament together, gaining a wider perspective on citizenship issues. Information and communication technology opportunities continue to develop and are expected to be a sustained area of growth through work with a jointly funded E-Learning Director. Bay Tree considers that an opportunity for access to that level of strategic planning would have been impossible with the funding available for it as a small special school.

Bay Tree's identity as a special school has been enhanced through recognition by mainstream colleagues of Bay Tree's strengths; a desire by mainstream colleagues to capitalise on Bay Tree's knowledge, skills and understanding of SEN issues and responding to them; and by the acceptance of Bay Tree as a professional equal instead of an 'add-on'.

The federation has been an 'organic' organisation and is expected to continue as such after funding ends. It is regarded as multi-school, multi-student and multi-dimensional. Flexibility has been inherent with different combinations of institutions buying into services according to their needs. Psychological and social benefits seem to have outweighed the financial and staffing level gains first identified.

temporary, part-time and dual-registered placements'; and 'work with schools to develop and agree a policy on outreach, particularly where resources have been delegated for this purpose' (ibid.: 3).

Funding arrangements for special schools are said to need to be sufficiently flexible to

- deliver an appropriate curriculum for all pupils;
- respond to changes in need for the pupil population;
- support integration and dual placements in mainstream schools and settings;
- provide short-term 'inreach' for some specific needs and pupils; and
- provide outreach support and training for those working in mainstream schools.

(ibid.: 31)

LEA funding to improve special schools

LEA funding to improve special schools includes investment in building and refurbishing or to develop or extend their provision and services. (See, for example, Boxes 10.3 and 10.4.)

Funding and dual placements between special and mainstream schools

Where there are dual placements and dual registration of pupils between a special school and a mainstream school, it is important that funding arrangements are clear to all concerned. (See, for example, Box 10.5.)

Box 10.3 KIRKLEES LA

Kirklees carried out a reorganisation of its special schools in 2006–7 to seek to ensure that the schools had high quality, suitable accommodation and facilities appropriate to the needs of the pupils and staff. The LA invested £4 million in the financial year 2004–5 on general reorganisation work and on specific work on special schools. It planned to spend a further £25 million for three new special schools.

Box 10.4 WIRRAL LA

Wirral LA successfully bid for over £350,000 government funding to develop extra-curricular and out-of-hours activities. In 2005, this involved eight of the LA's twelve special schools, as well as mainstream schools. From 2002–5, £90,000 was allocated from the LA standards fund to help special schools develop inclusion projects.

Funding arrangements for outreach and other services

The document *Inclusion: The Impact of LEA Support and Outreach Services* (OfSTED, 2005c) indicates some of the issues for special schools concerning outreach.

The quality and quantity of services were found to be variable partly because LEAs chose whether or not funding for support services was delegated to mainstream schools when these might choose to use the funding for other purposes (ibid.: para. 3). The report recommends that LAs 'consider wherever possible delegating the funding for support services to suitable special schools within a region in order that they can deliver the services to mainstream schools on an outreach basis' (ibid.: recommendations, p. 4).

The cost to LAs of non-maintained and independent school fees

In 2004, guidance for local authorities, *The Management of SEN Expenditure* (DfES, 2004d) (www.teachernet.gov.uk/senexpenditure) announced that the DfES was recruiting a number of 'SEN Expert Advisers' (ibid.: 7) to work with local authorities in the area of managing expenditure. In the context of expenditure on non-maintained and independent special school fees the document made various recommendations such as that local authorities 'under-

Box 10.5 HEXHAM PRIORY SCHOOL, NORTHUMBERLAND

Funding and dual registration

Hexham Priory School, Hexham, Northumberland is a co-educational community special school for 58 pupils aged 3 to 19 with severe learning difficulties or profound and multiple learning difficulties with some pupils having autistic spectrum disorder.

It has been organising dual placement for pupils since 1995 and at the time of writing several pupils have dual registration/placement with Priory and their local first or middle school. The main purpose is to provide pupils with access to the specialist teaching and resources at Priory while they also attend their local mainstream school. Pupils are often timetabled to do literacy and numeracy activities in the proportion of their time at Priory. A coordinator works with the mainstream school concerned preparing an Individual Education Plan for dually registered pupils and attending annual reviews. Pupils are supported on a one-to-one basis in mainstream schools by a teaching assistant who may be either a member of Priory School or the mainstream school staff depending on what best meets the needs of the individual pupil. Decisions on dual registration are made according to individual circumstances. Some pupils have started their education at Priory and become dual registered at Key Stage 2. Others have started in mainstream school and moved to dual registration with Priory when the curriculum becomes more challenging.

The funding of the dual registration at Priory developed in discussions with Northumberland County Council who agreed that any child attending Priory for between 0.1 and 0.4 full-time equivalent (fte) would be funded at 0.5 fte rate. Any child attending for between 0.5 fte and full-time would be treated as full-time for funding purposes. These arrangements allow Priory School flexibility to work with children when they are in the school and allow the school to maintain the quality of its support to mainstream staff working with the children.

take a corporate audit of unmet need and look at ways in which they can increase local capacity, working with social services and health through the Children and Young Persons Strategic Partnership (CYPSP) or Children's Trust' (ibid.: 2).

The guidance also states, 'By emphasising prevention and early intervention and building local capacity, high cost placements should be avoidable in all but the most exceptional circumstances' (ibid.: 24).

Box 10.6 BARRS COURT SCHOOL, HEREFORD

Barrs Court School, Hereford (www.barrscourt.hereford.sch.uk) is a co-educational community day school educating 56 pupils aged 11 to 19 years with moderate, severe or profound learning difficulties, some of whom have behavioural, emotional and social difficulties; autistic spectrum disorder; or multiple sensory impairment.

Prior to the appointment of a new head teacher in the spring of 2003 accommodation at the school had deteriorated, being described as unsatisfactory when the school was inspected under OfSTED in 2004. In addition to the poor state of the accommodation, the school was significantly over capacity and facing a large influx of children with profound and multiple learning difficulties for whom it lacked appropriate care and therapy facilities.

In the absence of capital investment from the local authority, the school decided to fund the cost of renovations via voluntary means. During 2004–5 the head teacher publicised the school's situation via the local media and made a series of presentations to local business and community groups from which emerged a small group of local business and community leaders keen to assist the school either directly as part of a fund-raising committee, or indirectly through supplying services such as printing.

In due course the decision was taken to establish a registered charity and charitable business with which to fund the demolishing of a derelict building at the rear of the school and build a new extension in which would be housed a hydrotherapy pool; intimate care and changing room facilities; an interactive performing arts studio; a store and a display area. It was agreed from the outset these new facilities would be available for community use beyond the school day and that the charity would continue to fund-raise once the new facilities were in place to facilitate their use out of school hours. As a consequence the Hydrosense Charitable Organisation (the 'Hydrosense Appeal') was founded.

Advice about the documentation required for registration was given free of charge from a local solicitor who had declared an interest in the proposed charity, and a Board of Trustees was elected, which included strong representation from the local business community, complemented by parents and governors from the school. In its first year of operation (2005–6) the charity raised over £500,000 towards the £750,000 target and the school anticipated the total amount would be reached before the end of 2006.

Income comes from an ongoing schedule of charitable events, local bequests, donations and grants from other charitable organisations. An unanticipated bonus associated with the Hydrosense Appeal has been the development of a network of local businesses keen to support the work of their local special school and enrich provision for pupils accordingly.

Forming a charitable organisation in a special school to assist fund-raising

A special school may decide to form a charitable organisation to aid funding for certain projects (as indicated in the Barrs Court case study – see Box 10.6).

Liaison between the head teacher, governors and bursar

With very wide opportunities for funding from different sources and for different purposes, it is essential that a special school have effective financial monitoring procedures and evaluation mechanisms in place to help ensure that funds are being used as efficiently as possible.

The school bursar may be based in a large special school or may be employed pro rata part-time by several employers including special schools. The duties of the bursar and his or her priorities need to be agreed with the head teacher and governors so that the school is fully informed of its financial state while the bursar understands the school's priorities. Regular liaison between the head teacher and bursar are one way of assisting this.

Thinking points

Readers may wish to consider with reference to a particular special school:

- the benefits and constraints of their general funding status (foundation, community, non-maintained, independent) and any opportunities for more effective use of funding;
- the extent to which opportunities for government funding are worth pursuing balancing the benefits and constraints that may be associated with them;
- where the special school is maintained by an LA the extent and fairness of LA funding for refurbishment, rebuilding, and extension of services;
- whether the school wishes to develop charitable trusts for particular projects.

Key text

DfES (2004d) *The Management of SEN Expenditure* (LEA/0149/2004) London, DfES. This document gives information and suggests approaches for LEAs to manage SEN expenditure. It may also be viewed on www.teachernet.gov.uk/sen expenditure. Its chapters include 'Independent and non-maintained special schools' (Chapter 3) and 'Maintained special schools and additionally resourced provision' (Chapter 4).

Spanish week 2

Conclusion

Promoting the special school

Previous chapters having examined areas in which special schools pursue excellence, this conclusion looks at ways in which the modern special school is promoted. I consider organisations and groups to which special schools might look for support and representation: national organisations; regional organisations; local authorities and local parents' groups; and organisations responsible for groups of independent and non-maintained special schools. The chapter also considers ways in which the special school itself can draw attention to its achievements though the press, radio and television, and the school's own publicity. The school profile and prospectus are mentioned.

Organisations supporting or representing special schools

National organisations

Rescare (www.rescare.org.uk), a national society for children and adults with learning disabilities and their families, campaigns for the retention and development of special schools. Run by families for families, it represents thousands of families and has affiliations in New Zealand and Australia.

The National Association for Independent Schools and Non-maintained Special Schools (NASS) (www.nasschools.org.uk) represents the provision for the considerable number of pupils educated in independent and non-maintained special schools. In the year 2005, in the Department for Education and Skills Statistics First Release (www.dfes.gov.uk/rsgateway/DB/SFR) there were 4,870 pupils on the roll of non-maintained special schools (SFR 24/2005 Table 1b). A further 6,290 pupils with statements were educated in independent special schools (SFR 24/2005 Table 2 'Children with Statements in January 2005' (f)). The total educated in the two types of school was therefore 11,160.

NASS has provided evidence of the quality of independent and mainstream special schools. In 2004, a pilot study involved the DfES working with 185 schools, including 35 special schools, to calculate value added for pupils' progress. Two special schools, The Mary Hare Grammar School for the Deaf, Berkshire (a non-maintained school) and RNIB New College, Worcester (an independent school) were first and second respectively for value added from KS2 to KS4 for the whole pilot (NASS, 2005a). Secondary School Achievement and Attainment tables 2004, for value added from KS2 to 15 years, indicated that 18 non-maintained NASS member schools achieved progress placing them in the top 5 per cent of schools (NASS, 2005b).

In 2004, data from OfSTED reports that were then current indicated the quality of education in 85 approved independent schools for pupils' progress and achievement, quality of teaching and learning, and the curriculum. In 78 per cent all standards were satisfactory or better, suggesting a positive picture for most but showing that too large a percentage were unsatisfactory in these areas. Similar data in 2005 for 63 non-maintained special schools indicated that in practically all, standards were satisfactory or better.

The DfES, in 2006, proposed providing start-up funds for a national representative body for special schools to be set up by NASS and the National Association of Emotional and Behavioural Difficulty schools. The aim was to allow a collective voice for special schools; offer additional training to special school staff; share best practice; and help special schools work more closely with mainstream schools for the inclusion of pupils with SEN.

In December 2005, the National Association of Special Educational Needs (www.nasen.org.uk) changed its acronym from NASEN to 'nasen' to indicate its commitment to inclusion. Its institutional members include special schools.

Gloucestershire Special School Protection League (www.gsspl.org.uk) launched a national campaign to 'prevent the culling of special schools in the name of inclusion'. Its Internet site has links to other organisations supporting special schools. The Voice of Independent Parents in Special Educational Needs (www.vips-in-sen.co.uk), a parents action group, aims to 'protect the decreasing number of excellent special schools'.

Regional organisations

The Regional Partnerships (formerly the SEN Regional Partnerships) cannot be said to specifically support or represent special schools but special schools have been involved in some of the work carried out by the partnerships and therefore other special schools may find reports of this work relevant.

Regional Partnerships seek to 'promote inclusion and positive outcomes for children with SEN and/or disabilities and looked after children' (*Regional Partnership News*, Spring 2006, 6: 1). They work by bringing partners together voluntarily to allow the national and regional sharing of good practice; supporting areas of national policy; working with government offices regarding regional priorities; and supporting the development of more inclusive policies and practices (DfES/The Regional Partnerships, 2006: 4, paraphrased).

Examples of the work of regional partnerships include the development of guidance on outreach by the then West SEN Regional Partnership mentioned in Chapter 2 'Clear Roles'. The West Midlands partnership has worked on autism and on mediation services between parents and the LA. Yorkshire and Humberside have made contributions to multi-agency working. The Eastern Region has worked on SEN officer accredited training leading to Business and Technical Education Council awards. In the South East, the South Central (SCRIP) and the South East (SERSEN) have developed protocols on joint working between local authorities and independent and non-maintained special schools.

The website www.teachernet.gov.uk/sen provides a link to 'The Regional Partnerships' which in turn lead to the sites of the particular partnerships.

Local authorities and local parent groups

LAs that support their special schools include Staffordshire, where a Targeted Capital Fund bid has been made for a new secondary special school and for a community vocational centre. Various working groups reflect the involvement of special schools in the work of the LA, for example a 'Challenging Needs' group including the head teachers of special schools was formed after the building of three enhanced units attached to special schools for pupils who might otherwise have been educated outside the county.

In Reading LA, special schools and the skills of their staff are publicly acknowledged. One school was refurbished in 2005 and another with aging buildings was to be replaced with a new special school in 2007.

Kirklees sees inclusion as concerning how young people feel about themselves and how they are motivated to participate in school and in wider society. Therefore, in determining how 'included' a pupil is the LA believes that where a child attends school and whether it is a special or mainstream school is less important than the experiences he has. The LA has plans to spend £25 million for three new special schools.

Hampshire LA supports its 28 special schools through, among other things, a commitment to their continuation and development as schools in their own right, not as revolving doors or holding stations awaiting mainstream school transformation. Many other LAs also offer strong support for their special schools (Farrell, 2006f).

Local groups include parents fighting to save the Kingsdown School, Eastwood, Essex (www.kingsdownparents.co.uk); parents resisting special school closures in Leicester (www.saveourschools.co.uk); a group against the London Borough of Bromley and the LA over inclusion for children with SEN until the child can cope and there is parental agreement (www.sen-action.com); parents of pupils at Winchelsea School, Poole, Dorset, fighting closure by the LA (www.spiritofwinchelsea.co.uk); and the Dudley Special School Protection League (www.dsspl.co.uk).

Organisations responsible for groups of independent and non-maintained special schools

Many independent and non-maintained schools are run individually. In some instances, larger bodies oversee several schools and these bodies may carry out other work too.

Regarding non-maintained schools, various charities run several special schools. Barnardos (www.barnardos.org.uk) administers High Close School, Wokingham, Wiltshire; Spring Hill School, Ripon, North Yorkshire; and Meadows School, Southborough, Kent. I CAN (www.ican.org.uk) runs Dawn House School, Mansfield, Nottinghamshire and Meath School, Surrey. The National Autistic Society (www.nas.org.uk) is the umbrella body for Radlett Lodge School, Hertfordshire; The Sybil Elgar School, Middlesex and several other special schools. The charity National Children's Homes (www.nch. org.uk) is responsible for Penhurst School, Chipping Norton; and Westwood School, Broadstairs, Kent. The Royal National Institute for the Blind (RNIB) (www.rnib.org.uk) has three special schools in England including: RNIB Rushton Hall School and Children's Home, Coventry and New College Worcester.

An umbrella group sometimes administers several independent schools. Priory Education Services (www.priorygroup.com) is responsible for colleges of further education and several schools including Eastwood Grange School, Derbyshire; and North Hill House, Somerset. Scope, (www.scope.org.uk) an organisation whose focus is people with cerebral palsy, supports Meldreth Manor School, Hertfordshire; Ingfield Manor School, West Sussex; Rutland House School, Nottingham; and Beech Tree School, Preston. The Hesley Group (www.hesleygroup.co.uk) oversees several special schools including Southlands School, Hampshire; and Fullerton House School, Doncaster, South Yorkshire.

Publicity and the special school

This section discusses ways in which the special school can manage publicity and raise its positive profile in the community. I consider local newspapers, local radio and regional television, and how publicity may be used to enhance the school's local presence.

The press

Consider the following opening to a press release from a fictitious special school for its local newspaper (see Box C.1).

Newspapers (and other media) are particularly attracted to human-interest stories. So a special school wanting to convey, for example, the results of its recent accreditation and examination successes or other data may find it

---

Box C.1 PRESS RELEASE 1

Rosebank Special School students achieved very well in recent examinations. Of the ten students who entered for . . . (the results follow).

Box C.2 PRESS RELEASE 2

After fifteen years working at Rosebank Special School, teacher Jane Thomas said goodbye to pupils, staff and parents at a supper held at the school to mark her retirement. In her speech, she said how much the school had changed and improved over the years she had been there. 'This year the examination results are the best I can remember', she told the audience. 'Ten students were entered for . . . ' (the results follow).

---

difficult to do so through the press. However, the two can be combined in many ways as the second attempt indicates (see Box C.2).

Such a press release, although it could no doubt be improved further, stands a much better chance of capturing the interest of readers and therefore of the editor. A study of the content of the paper will suggest whether there might be room for a news story of a feature on the school or an aspect of its work. The writer of the press release should take care to study the style of the newspaper and emulate it closely.

Other human-interest stories will involve pupils speaking of their own achievements: academic, extra-curricular, personal and social; staff talking of changes or new developments in the school; parents telling of how they support the school and the aspects they value (perhaps at a parents' meeting).

The school should check with the editor first but, if it can take good quality photographs of the size and type that newspapers say they need and offer them with a press release, this is likely to increase the chances of the press release being used. The newspaper may want black and white photographs or may ask for digital pictures to be e-mailed to its offices. Of course, the newspaper may prefer to send its own photographer to an event so it is worth ascertaining what the paper prefers.

As the special school establishes a certain expertise, the local press and others may approach it for background advice and information on special educational needs more generally. Special schools should be very careful not to respond in a way that can be distorted or used out of context. A response to a general query might be to make a note of the reporter's details and agree to telephone him back within an agreed time. This gives the school time to put its views in writing and fax them to the newspaper so that there can be no misunderstanding as well as providing time to check facts and reflect on the response.

If the special school is LA-maintained, there may be guidance from the LA about how to respond to such enquiries. In any event the school should make it clear when it is giving its own opinion and when it is speaking with the agreement of the LA. Although it may not be feasible for a special school to have its own press officer, several special schools or other clusters of schools may decide to fund a post of press officer to represent and promote them.

Radio

A script prepared by a special school for local radio will need to capture human interest just as a newspaper story does. For anyone not used to writing a radio script, it will be helpful to listen to the station carefully and transcribe one or two features to help pick up the style including the length of utterances, the vocabulary used and the sort of features that tend to appeal. The script might be an item of news or an announcement about a forthcoming concert or other event held by the school but it is still important to write it in a style that is already used by the station concerned.

Another contact with local radio can come through inviting technicians to record a concert or musical work at the school. Given professional equipment and expertise, the school might record its own material and send the tapes to the local radio for consideration, although it is usually better to check what the station wants first.

Television

Teachers' TV, (www.teachers.tv) an editorially independent television channel broadcasting on digital, cable and satellite, is funded by the DfES. Education Digital, a consortium of Brook Lapping, Independent Television and the Institute of Education, London, undertakes programme production and management. It provides several examples of the work of special schools.

For a particular special school, it is likely that regional television is a point of contact. For a big important event, television may be interested. A key aspect, so obvious that it may be overlooked, is that ideally the event should be very visual. Something needs to be happening that justifies a television camera and crew being there rather than a newspaper reporter or a radio presenter.

In the same way that the school analyses the topics covered by a local newspaper, the requirements of local television should be ascertained by studying the sorts of programme slots that might form a platform for your event, whether this is news or a feature programme. What is happening that is *visually* interesting? When is it going to happen? What arrangements are necessary for the crew to get their equipment in place? Practicalities need to be known in advance to make the event and the coverage run smoothly.

If a speech is made, it is helpful for the television company to have a copy with the likely timing so that if they want to catch a particular segment, they will be ready. Given this it is important that the speaker keeps closely to the script.

Using publicity to raise the school's local presence

The easiest medium to have on constant display is the printed medium. Having achieved a good write-up in the local press, the school will wish to make it known by displaying the articles, quoting with permission from them in school literature, drawing the attention of parents, LA officers and others to the coverage.

Some schools have a display of press cuttings on a notice board or in a book kept in the foyer. If cuttings are to be fresh-looking, the school may buy several copies of a newspaper, displaying one and keeping the others in a dark place so they do not become discoloured by sunlight then replacing the display cutting as necessary.

The school's evidence of its recent achievements is also a good source of publicity. Foyers, classrooms, corridors can be used to display photographs. For special occasions, for example on parents' evenings, the school can show off its achievements through audiotapes (of the school's own making or copies of radio broadcasts) or videotapes/DVDs (the school's own or copies of television broadcasts).

The school's literature, such as its prospectus, will be carefully presented to show in an interesting way the school's strengths as well as giving necessary basic information. The school's website also provides the opportunity to use text, photographs, video clips and other forms of display to show what the school does. Quotations from the school's most recent OfSTED report and, where the school has boarding provision, the latest Commission for Social Care (CSCI) inspection report may be used with links to the full report.

The school's Internet site can be managed and kept up-to-date to effectively present the school's achievements to the local community and beyond. (See, for example, Box C.3.)

A well-produced DVD of the school's work can help present a clear picture of what the special school does. For example, the DVD for New Rush Hall School, Redbridge (www.nrhs.redbridge.sch.uk) includes interviews with pupils and parents expressing appreciation of what the school does as well as examples of the school's work and views of staff.

The school 'profile' and the school prospectus

Following the Education Act 2005, governing bodies of maintained schools (except nursery schools) no longer have to produce a governors' annual report, which has been replaced by a school profile that can be completed by schools

Box C.3 WEBSITE DEVELOPMENTS AT EXHALL GRANGE SCHOOL AND SCIENCE COLLEGE

The approach used by Exhall Grange School and Science College (EGSSC), Warwickshire provides pointers to how websites might be developed and some of the issues that arise. In developing its website, EGSSC had several meetings with teaching staff, the LEA and technicians about the development of its website. EGSSC ensured it was clear about what it wanted the website to facilitate. It consulted with parents, using a questionnaire, about whether they can easily access the Internet and what features they would find most useful to them. It drew a new specification for the site considering the following:

- How should basic information about the school be made available?
- What would this basic information consist of?
- Should we use the website for transitory information, like homework?
- If so how do we input this information?
- How can parents find out more about the syllabus/curriculum that their child is following?
- Should there be 'open access', should access to the entire site be user-name and password controlled or should access to personal areas be the only areas requiring permissions?
- Should there be a way for students to access their personal areas of the network remotely via the website?
- Should there be a way for parents to access their child's personal areas?
- Should the school communicate with parents electronically through the secure areas of the website as well as using paper? and
- Should the site provide links to other organisations? If so, which?

and published on the Internet. Consequently, as an annual update on the work of the school a well-drafted school profile has assumed importance (www.teachernet.gov.uk/management/newrelationship/schoolprofile/). The part that is already filled in ('pre-populated' to use the jargon) by the Department for Education and Skills concerns standards and the profile has to give a summary of the latest OfSTED report, but the other sections give the opportunity to present what the school does well and its future plans. Headings completed by the school including 'what have been our successes this year?' and 'how do we make sure that our pupils are healthy, safe and well supported?' provide a good opportunity for the special school to emphasise its strengths. Links may also be made to other online information the school has, such as details of after-school clubs. A template is available (http://schoolprofile.teachernet. gov.uk).

Changes to requirements for the school's prospectus open up opportunities for the special school to present the strongest features of provision along with statutory requirements such as details of existing facilities to assist access to the school by pupils with disabilities (www.teachernet.gov.uk/management/ newrelationship/schoolprofile/).

A final word

This book has examined issues relating to special schools that are likely to influence decisions the schools make for the foreseeable future. These concerned: organisation and structure, outreach and other roles, training for special school staff, the development of distinctive provision, children's well-being, target setting, multi-professional working, home–school partnerships, pupil participation, and suitable funding as well as in this conclusion looking at ways in which the special school can be promoted.

I hope that the suggestions and examples provided are helpful to special schools; not only in England, but elsewhere as they continue to develop and the role of special schools becomes increasingly appreciated. Pupils educated in good special schools and those aspiring to have such an education; their parents; professionals working in and supporting special schools and others are all contributing to the continued strengthening of special schools. Special schools have no cause to be complacent – and neither are they – because they have a duty to improve their work and continually strive for excellence.

Key text

(Annually) *Writers' and Artists' Yearbook*, London, A&C Black.
> This gives useful addresses including those for BBC regional television and local radio; independent regional television; and independent local radio.

Bibliography

Adey, P. and Shayer, M. (2002) *Learning Intelligence*, Buckingham, Open University Press.

Aitken, S. and Millar, S. (2002) *Listening to Children with Communication Support Needs*, Glasgow, Sense Scotland.

Appleton, P. L. and Minchcom, P. E. (1991) 'Models of parent partnership and child development centres', *Child: Care, Health and Development*, 17: 27–38.

Assessment Reform Group (1999) *Assessment for Learning: Beyond the Black Box*, Cambridge, School of Education University of Cambridge.

Beatie, R. (2006) *Guidance on the New Strand of Specialist Schools Programme for Special Schools*, London, DfES (see also www.standards.dfes.gov.uk/specialschools to view the application procedure).

Black, P., Harrison, C., Lee, C., Marshall, B. and William, D. (2002) *Working Inside the Black Box*, London, Kings College London.

Blagg, N., Ballinger, M., Gardener, R., Petty, M. and Williams, G. (1988) *Somerset Thinking Skills Course*, Oxford, Blackwell/Somerset County Council.

Carpenter, B. (ed.) (1997) *Families in Context: Emerging Trends in Family Support and Early Intervention*, London, David Fulton Publishers.

—— (2001) 'Enabling Partnership: Families and Schools', in B. Carpenter, R. Ashdown and K. Bovair (eds), *Enabling Access: Effective Teaching and Learning for Pupils with Learning Difficulties* (2nd edn), London, David Fulton Publishers.

Cunningham, C. and Davis, H. (1985) *Working with Parents: Frameworks for Collaboration*, Buckingham, Open University Press.

Dale, N. (1996) *Working with Families of Children with Special Needs*, London, Routledge.

Department for Education and Employment (1997) *Excellence for All Children: Meeting Special Educational Needs*, London, DfEE.

—— (2001) *Supporting the Target Setting Process (revised March 2001): Guidance for Effective Target Setting for Pupils with Special Educational Needs*, London, DfEE.

—— Qualifications and Curriculum Authority (2001) *Planning, Teaching and Assessing the Curriculum for Pupils with Learning Difficulties: General Guidelines*, London, DfEE/QCA.

Department for Education and Skills (2001a) *Special Educational Needs Code of Practice*, London, DfES.

—— (2001b) *Inclusive Schooling: Children with Special Educational Needs*, London, DfES.

—— (2001c) *The Distribution of Resources to Support Inclusion*, London, DfES.

—— (2002) *An Introduction to Extended Schools – Providing Opportunities and Services to All*, London, DfES.

—— (2003a) *Data Collection by Type of Special Educational Needs*, London, DfES.

—— (2003b) *Developing the Role of School Support Staff: What the National Agreement Means for You*, London, DfES.

—— (2003c) *The Report of the Special Schools Working Group*, London, DfES.

—— (2004a) *A Guide to the Law for School Governors: Community Schools (Including Community Special Schools)*, London, DfES.

—— (2004b) *A Guide to the Law for School Governors: Foundation Schools (Including Foundation Special Schools)*, London, DfES.

—— (2004c) *Removing Barriers to Achievement: The Government's Strategy for SEN*, London, DfES.

—— (2004d) *The Management of SEN Expenditure* (LEA/0149/2004), London, DfES.

—— (2005) *Multi Agency Working – Introduction and Overview (Every Child Matters: Change for Children)*, London, DfES. (www.ecm.gov/multiagencyworking/).

—— and Department of Health (2004) *National Service Framework for Children, Young People and Maternity Services: Supporting Local Delivery*, London, DfES/DoH.

—— /Partnership UK (2005c) *Schools PFI – Post-Signature Review by Partnerships UK for the Department for Education and Skills* (Phase 2 Report, May), London, DfES/Partnership UK.

—— /Regional Partnerships (2006) *Regional Partnerships: Who We Are and What We Do*, London, DfES.

Department of Education and Science (1978) *Special Educational Needs – Report of the Committee of Enquiry into the Education of Handicapped Children and Young People (The Warnock Report)*, London, Her Majesty's Stationery Office.

Doran, C. and Cameron, R. J. (1995) 'Learning about learning: metacognitive approaches in the classroom', *Educational Psychology in Practice*, 11 (2): 15–23.

Dyson, A., Lyn, M. and Millward, A. (1998) *Effective Communication Between Schools, LEAs, Health and Social Services in the Field of Special Educational Needs*, London, DfEE.

Ellis, T. (1984) 'Extending the school year and day', ERIC Clearing House on Educational Management, *ERIC Digest*, 7: 1–3.

Farrell, M. (2005) *Key Issues in Special Education: Raising Standards of Pupils' Attainment and Achievement*, London, Routledge.

—— (2006a) *The Effective Teacher's Guide to Behavioural, Emotional and Social Difficulties*, London, Routledge.

—— (2006b) *The Effective Teacher's Guide to Moderate, Severe and Profound Learning Difficulties*, London, Routledge.

—— (2006c) *The Effective Teacher's Guide to Dyslexia and Other Specific Learning Difficulties*, London, Routledge.

—— (2006d) *The Effective Teacher's Guide to Autism and Other Communication Difficulties*, London, Routledge.

—— (2006e) *The Effective Teacher's Guide to Sensory Impairment and Physical Disability*, London, Routledge.

—— (2006f) *Celebrating the Special School*, London, David Fulton Publishers.

Feuerstein, R. (1979) *The Dynamic Assessment of Retarded Performers: The Learning Potential Assessment Device; Theory, Instruments and Techniques*, Baltimore: MD, University Park Press.

Feuerstein, R., Rand, Y., Hoffman, M. B. and Miller, R. (1980) *Instrumental Enrichment: An Intervention Programme for Cognitive Modifiability*, Baltimore: MD, University Park Press.

Fisher, R. (1998) *Teaching Thinking: Philosophical Enquiry in the Classroom*, London, Cassell.

Flutter, J. and Rudduck, J. (2004) *Consulting Pupils: What's in it for Schools?*, London, Routledge-Falmer.

Glynne-Rule, L. (1995) 'Support for the disabled', *Times Educational Supplement*, April.

Greenwood, C. (2002) *Understanding the Needs of Parents: Guidelines for Effective Collaboration with Parents of Children with Special Educational Needs*, London, David Fulton Publishers.

Gunton, P. (1990) 'Encouraging self advocacy at an early age', dissertation to Cambridge University Institute of Education.

Hart, R. A. (1997) *Children's Participation: The Theory and Practice of Involving Young Citizens in Community Development and Environmental Care*, London, Earthscan Publications.

Henggeler, S. (1999) 'Multi-systemic therapy: an overview of clinical procedures, outcomes and policy implications', *Child Psychology and Psychiatry Review*, 4 (1): 2–10.

Hornby, G. (1995) *Working with Parents of Children with Special Needs*, London, Cassell.

—— (2003) 'Counselling and Guidance of Parents', in G. Hornby, E. Hall and C. Hall (eds), *Counselling Pupils in Schools: Skills and Strategies for Teachers*, London, Routledge-Falmer, pp. 129–40.

House of Commons Education and Skills Committee (2006) *Special Educational Needs: Third Report of Session 2005–6 Volume 1*, London, The Stationery Office.

I-CAN (2001) *Joint Professional Framework for All Teachers and Speech and Language Therapists Working with Speech, Language and Communication Needs*, London, I-CAN.

Jelly, M., Fuller, A. and Byers, R. (2000) *Involving Pupils in Practice: Promoting Partnerships with Pupils with Special Educational Needs*, London, David Fulton.

Kirby, A. and Drew, S. (2003) *Guide to Dyspraxia and Developmental Coordination Disorders*, London, David Fulton Publishers.

Lake, M. and Needham, M. (1990) *Top Ten Thinking Skills*, Birmingham, The Questions Publishing Company.

Lansdown, G. (1995) *Taking Part: Children's Participation in Decision Making*, London, Institute for Public Policy Research.

Lawson, H. (1996) 'Exploring the relationship between teaching, assessment and research methodology: an enquiry into pupil involvement with pupils who experience severe learning difficulties', unpublished Ph.D. thesis, University of East Anglia.

Layzell, P. (1995) 'Case study of a school–parent liaison programme', *Therapeutic Care and Education*, 4 (2): 3–31.

Lewis, A. (2004) 'And when did you last see your father? Exploring the views of children with learning difficulties/disabilities', *British Journal of Special Education*, 31 (3): 3–9.

Lipman, M., Sharp, A. and Oscanyan, F. (1980) *Philosophy in the Classroom*, Princeton, Temple University Press.

Marchant, R. and Cross, M. (2002) *How It Is*, London, The National Society for the Prevention of Cruelty to Children.

McGuinness, C. (1999) *From Thinking Skills to Thinking Classrooms: Research Brief No. 115*, London, Department for Education and Skills.

Middleton, L. (1998) 'Consumer satisfaction with services for disabled children', *Journal of Interprofessional Care*, 12 (2): 223–31.

Mirfin-Veitch, B. and Bray, A. (1997) 'Grandparents: Part of the Family', in B. Carpenter (ed.), *Families in Context: Emerging Trends in Family Support and Early Intervention*, London, David Fulton Publishers.

Mittler, P. (2001) 'Preparing for Self-Advocacy', in B. Carpenter, R. Ashdown and K. Bovair (eds), *Enabling Access: Effective Teaching and Learning for Pupils with Learning Difficulties* (2nd edn), London, David Fulton Publishers.

——— and Mittler, H. (1994) *Innovations in Family Support for People with Learning Difficulties*, Lancashire, Lisieux Hall.

Mosley, J. (1996) *Quality Circle Time*, Wisbech, Learning Development Aids.

Murris, K. and Haynes, J. (2000) *Storywise: Thinking Through Picture Books*, Somerset, Dialogue Works.

National Association for Non-Maintained and Independent Schools (2005a) *Pace and Progression Pilot – Achievement and Attainment Tables 2004*, London, NASS.

——— (2005b) *Secondary School Achievement Tables 2004*, London, NASS.

National Remodelling Team (2004) *Planning, Preparation and Assessment Strategies – Overview and Toolkit/Time for Standards – Transforming the School Workforce*, London, DfES.

Newport, F. (2004) *Outreach Support from Special Schools*, Taunton, South West SEN Regional Partnership.

Office for Standards in Education (2004) *Setting Targets for Pupils with Special Educational Needs* (HMI 751), London, OfSTED.

——— (2005a) *Every Child Matters: Framework for the Inspection of Schools in England from September 2005* (HMI 2435), London, OfSTED.

——— (2005b) *Using the Evaluation Schedule: Guidance for Inspectors of Schools*, London, OfSTED.

——— (2005c) *Inclusion: The Impact of LEA Support and Outreach Services* (HMI 2452), London, OfSTED.

——— (2005d) *Conducting the Inspection: Guidance for Inspectors of Schools* (HMI 2502), London, OfSTED.

——— (2006) *Inclusion: Does it matter where pupils are taught? Provision and Outcomes for Pupils with Learning Difficulties and Disabilities* (HMI 2535), London, OfSTED.

Panter, S. 'Mathematics', in B. Carpenter, R. Ashdown and K. Bovair (eds), *Enabling Access: Effective Teaching and Learning for Pupils with Learning Difficulties* (2nd edn), London, David Fulton Publishers.

Qualifications and Curriculum Authority (1999) *Curriculum Guidance for the Foundation Stage*, London, QCA.

——— (2001a) *Planning, Teaching and Assessing the Curriculum for Pupils with Learning Difficulties: English*, London, QCA.

——— (2001b) *Planning, Teaching and Assessing the Curriculum for Pupils with Learning Difficulties: Science*, London, QCA.

Randall, P. and Parker, J. (1999) *Supporting the Families of Children with Autism*, Chichester, John Wiley.

Rinaldi, W. (1992/2001) *Social Use of Language Programme (SULP)*, Windsor, NFER-Nelson.

Romney, D. M. and Samuels, M. T. (2001) 'A meta-analytic evaluation of Feuerstein's instrumental enrichment programme', *Education and Child Psychology*, 18 (4): 19–34.

Rose, R. *et al.* (1996) 'Promoting the greater involvement of pupils with special needs in the management of their own assessment and learning process', *British Journal of Special Education*, 23: 166–71.

Rose, S. (2006) *A Handbook for Lunchtime Supervisors and their Managers*, London, David Fulton Publishers.

Sharon, H. and Coulter, M. (1994) *Changing Children's Minds: Feuerstein's Revolution in Teaching Intelligence*, Birmingham, Questions Publishing Company.

South West SEN Regional Partnership (2004) *Self Evaluation Framework for Outreach Providers*, Taunton, South West SEN Regional Partnership.

Steering Group for the Inspection of Children's Services (2004) *Every Child Matters: Joint Area Reviews of Children's Services*, London, SGICS.

Stone, J. (1997) 'Working with Families', in H. Mason and S. McCall (eds) with C. Arter, M. McLinden and J. Stone, *Visual Impairment: Access to Education for Children and Young People*, London, David Fulton Publishers.

Teacher Training Agency (1999) *National Special Educational Needs Specialist Standards*, London, TTA.

Training and Development Agency for Schools (2006a) *Professional Standards for Higher Level Teaching Assistants*, London, TDA.

—— (2006b) *Meeting the Standards for Higher Level Teaching Assistants: Handbook for Candidates*, London, TDA.

—— (2006c) *Meeting the Standards for Higher Level Teaching Assistants: Handbook for Providers of Preparation and Assessment*, London, TDA.

—— (2006d) *Guidance on the Standards for the Award of HLTA Status*, London, TDA.

Warnock, M. (2005) 'Special educational needs: a new look', *Impact No. 11*, London, The Philosophy of Education Society of Great Britain.

—— (2006) 'Foreword', in M. Farrell, *Celebrating the Special School*, London, David Fulton Publishers.

Watkins, C. (2001) *Learning about Learning Enhances Performance*, London, London University Institute of Education School Improvement Network (Research Matters Series No. 13).

Webster-Stratton, C. (1999) *How to Promote Children's Social and Emotional Competence*, London, Paul Chapman.

Whitbread, D. (1996) *Teaching and Learning in the Early Years*, London, Routledge.

Whittles, S. (1998) *Can You Hear Us? Including the Views of Disabled Children and Young People*, London, Save the Children.

Wilmott, D. (2006) 'Educational Inclusion and Special Schooling within a Local Authority', thesis submitted for the degree of Doctor in Education (EdD), University of Birmingham.

Addresses

B Squared
Burnhill Business Centre, Provident House, Burrell Row, High Street,
  Beckenham, Kent BR3 1AT
tel: 0208 249 6333
fax: 0208 249 6383
e-mail: info@bsquaredsen.co.uk
website: www.bsquaredsen.co.uk

Continyou provides The Extended School Support Service (TESSS) for
the Department for Education and Skills and organises a community
schools network
e-mail: extended.schools@continyou.org
website: www.continyou.org.uk

**National Association of Independent and Non-Maintained
Special Schools (NASS)**
PO Box 705, York YO30 6WW
tel/fax: 01845 522 542
e-mail: georginacarney@btinternet.com
website: www.nasschools.org.uk

The National Parent Partnership Network (NPPN)
Council for Disabled Children, 8 Wakeley Street, London EC1V
tel: 0207 843 6058

Office for Standards in Education
Alexandra House, 33 Kingsway, London WC2B 6SE
e-mail: schoolinspection@ofsted.gov.uk
School inspection help line, tel: 0207 421 6662
OfSTED Publications Centre, tel: 07002 637 833
fax: 07002 693 274

Performance Indicators for Value Added Target Setting (PIVATS)

Professional Support Team, Lancashire School Effectiveness Service,
   PO Box 51, County Hall, Preston PR1 8RJ
tel: 01772 531 525
e-mail: pivats@ed.lancscc.gov.uk
website: www.lancashire.gov.uk/education/pivats/services/intro1.asp

Qualification and Curriculum Authority

83 Piccadilly, London W1J 8QA
tel: 0207 509 5555
fax: 0207 509 6666
e-mail: info@qca.org.uk
website: www.qca.org.uk

Rescare

Rayner House, 23 Higher Hillgate, Stockport, Cheshire SK1 3ER
tel: 0161 474 7323
fax: 0161 480 3668
e-mail: office@rescare.org.uk
website: www.rescare.org.uk

SEN Regional Partnership (South West)

Bishops Hull House, Bishops Hull, Taunton TA1 5EP
tel: 01823 365 437

Teachernet

website: www.teachernet.gov.uk/wholeschool/extendedschools

The Voice of Independent Parents in Special Educational Needs

website: www.vips-in-sen.co.uk

Index

eBooks – at www.eBookstore.tandf.co.uk

A library at your fingertips!

eBooks are electronic versions of printed books. You can store them on your PC/laptop or browse them online.

They have advantages for anyone needing rapid access to a wide variety of published, copyright information.

eBooks can help your research by enabling you to bookmark chapters, annotate text and use instant searches to find specific words or phrases. Several eBook files would fit on even a small laptop or PDA.

NEW: Save money by eSubscribing: cheap, online access to any eBook for as long as you need it

Annual subscription packages

We now offer special low-cost bulk subscriptions to packages of eBooks in certain subject areas. These are available to libraries or to individuals.

For more information please contact webmaster.ebooks@tandf.co.uk

We're continually developing the eBook concept, so keep up to date by visiting the website.

www.eBookstore.tandf.co.uk